House Beautiful

CREATING
Children's Rooms

Libby Norman

NEW HOLLAND

Contents

Introduction

Decorating a child's room brings out the adventurer in us. Even parents who have never strayed below the safe neutrals section of the colour chart suddenly find themselves contemplating the relative merits of bubble gum and candy floss pink. There are the hours spent poring over wallpaper samples bedecked with wizard's castles, glittering galaxies or prowling wild animals, not to mention the hunt in stores and mail order catalogues to find perfect finishing touches for this magical kingdom.

And a child's room really is a magical kingdom. It is the place where great escapades are planned, inspired pictures are drawn and where he or she can be transported in an instant into a world of make believe. Designing a room your child loves living in is also a golden opportunity to nurture their imagination – and flex imaginative muscles of your own.

This book helps you make the most of the opportunity by guiding you through key decisions. You will find inspiring ideas backed by sound practical advice (even fairies and space explorers need storage and a comfortable bed!). Every chapter contains practical step-by-step projects – from decorating a nursery blanket, to revamping a wardrobe and masterminding paint effects on walls. All the projects are easy enough to tackle over a weekend, and there are simple ideas panels dotted throughout the book featuring inspirational projects that take an afternoon or less to complete.

If you are faced with four white walls – always a daunting prospect – then start with **Creative colour schemes** (pages 8–29). This shows you how to select exactly the right shades and patterns to make the most of your space, whatever its size or aspect. You will also find advice about mixing colours – including failsafe colour pairings and more daring contrasting combinations. **Layout, furniture and flooring** (pages 30–55) is devoted to essential shopping, safety and planning decisions – from selecting a bed to finding furniture that adapts as they grow and a floor tough enough to withstand boisterous games. A key section is devoted to getting the layout of furniture right, so that even small or awkwardly shaped rooms look balanced and allow your child more space for play.

Finding a home for all those toys and games is a subject close to every parent's heart, so **Simple storage and clever details** (pages 56–79) is packed with useful and accessible stowaway solutions, plus extra features that make a bedroom fun to live in. If you decide to take the decorating one stage further, **Themed rooms** (pages 80–105) shows you inspirational room ideas – from fairyland to space – and details how to put each look together and choose or make the extras that bring the themed setting to life.

Children's tastes change almost as fast as they grow, so **Make a bedroom into a den** (pages 106–19) gives pointers on adapting to changing needs, including revitalizing a decorating scheme by introducing more sophisticated elements. You will find advice on creating a comfortable home study space, as well as designing an environment where they can relax, pursue hobbies and entertain their friends.

However you decide to deck out your child's room, enjoy the adventure and the licence it gives you to be bold and creative. Along the way you may even recapture something of the magic of your own childhood.

▶ Use bold colours and patterns to bring a bedroom to life.

▶ Porthole murals give a below-decks flavour to a nautical room.

CHAPTER 1

creative colour schemes

Take inspiration from
a child's eye view of the world
and have fun with the colour card

Practical starting points

Faced with a mountain of colour cards or pattern books, the best starting point is to narrow down your choice to those that complement the room's shape, size, existing or fitted furniture, and aspect.

Work with your room shape

Make the most of your child's bedroom by choosing a scheme that suits both its shape and dimensions. Clever decorating can also create focal points and make an awkward space appear more balanced.

Square room

This is by far the easiest shape to work with, but if the room is small it can feel 'boxy' and cramped. You can add interest by painting or papering one wall in a different shade; this can create the illusion that the room is not completely square and adds a point of focus (see Wallpaper feature walls, page 17).

◀ *Dark paint turns a sloping ceiling into an interesting feature.*

▼ *Use colour to define an awkward corner and turn it into a useful study space.*

Choosing colours

Soft, understated colours may hold sway in the rest of your home, but children's rooms are the perfect excuse to suspend grown-up rules and have fun with the colour card. Children respond to vibrant shades, not taupe or magnolia, so if you let them decide on a colour scheme, be prepared for a dazzling combination. To avoid nasty surprises, set some parameters (see Children's choice, opposite), and bear in mind that this is a zone for restful sleep, as much as stimulating play. Remember, too, that although this is your child's space, you will also probably be spending a lot of time in here, so it pays to choose a scheme you can live with and adapt as your child's taste changes.

Continue the colour from the feature wall in furniture or accessories, for instance, a painted chair, rug or duvet cover.

Rectangular room

The trick here is to make the room feel more balanced, especially if the bed will only fit down the longer side of the rectangle. The easiest way to do this is to paint one or both the longer walls in paler shades – that way they will recede (see Use colour to enhance space, right), creating the illusion that the room is more evenly proportioned.

L-shaped room

An awkward corner is hard to incorporate, so turn it into a feature. For girls, this makes a perfect 'vanity zone' if you add a dressing table and mirror. Older children can utilize the space as a study or computer zone if you install a desk and proper task lighting. Define the area with paint or patterned paper, or hang cork pinboards so your child can decorate the space.

Decide what is staying

If the room is a blank canvas, you can take your pick of the colour card, but if some furnishings are staying, incorporate them at the outset. To do this, pick out existing colours somewhere else with accessories. For instance, if you are keeping the carpet, introduce the same shade in cushions, lampshades, picture frames or a duvet cover and then you can choose a different colour for the walls. Here are more tips to help you create a unified scheme:

- If fitted furniture or an existing carpet dominates a large area, keep the scheme simple and introduce no more than two additional colours for walls and woodwork.

- Toning shades often look more effective than harsh contrasts. If you are working with a strong colour such as red, consider choosing a pale shade of pink to complement it.

- If you are finding it difficult to find an exact colour match, look for patterned accessories rather than blocks of a single colour. You will find it much easier to get a convincing colour match.

- Introducing plenty of white or cream, either through patterns, or areas of neutral walls and woodwork, will help to harmonize your scheme.

USE COLOUR TO ENHANCE SPACE

Pale colours are often described as 'receding', which means they make spaces appear larger than they are, while deeper and warmer tones are 'advancing' colours. If the room is small and you want to create a feeling of space, choose from the lighter end of the spectrum. If you want to make a large room feel cosy, paint one or two walls in a richer shade.

CHILDREN'S CHOICE

The colour that appeals to a child given a free choice can be overwhelming when painted across all four walls, particularly if it is bright pink or orange. It is a good idea to let even very young children have a say in the decision-making – after all this is their room – but you will ensure longevity for the scheme if you set some guidelines. Here are some tried-and-trusted methods for ensuring that everybody loves the finished result:

- Get an idea of the sort of colours your child wants, then pre-select the shades that appeal to you and present your child with a shortlist. This means that he or she will make the final choice, and you get a colour you can live with.

- Allow your child to pick from the colour cards, but then combine their choice with other softer colours to make the finished result more bearable. The bright pink or orange he or she likes can be used to pick out details, such as a chair or toy box, or be restricted to one wall.

- Let your child make the first choice and then pick a paler shade from the same colour card. Two or three shades lighter will provide a similar effect, without the need for sunglasses.

▶ *Add stripes in harmonious shades to transform a plain pine wardrobe.*

Work with the space

Pick the right shade and pattern combinations to maximize natural assets – and minimize problem features. Here are some guidelines.

Small and low-ceiling rooms

🖌 Use pale or pastel colours as your base shade. Deeper shades can work if they are restricted to one or two walls or used as accent colours. They are particularly effective when used to emphasize an unusual feature, such as a sloping ceiling.

🖌 Avoid anything that cuts the room in two, e.g. wide, horizontal stripes. Vertical stripes are useful for making a low-ceilinged room feel taller but steer clear if the room is also narrow or they will emphasize its skinny proportions.

🖌 Choose a wallpaper design with a small pattern and avoid introducing too many 'busy' patterns on carpets and soft furnishings or they will overwhelm the space.

Large and high-ceiling rooms

🖌 Choose warm colours and break up large areas of wall with patterns, shelves or pictures.

🖌 Paint the ceiling one or two shades darker than the walls to make a very tall room feel less lofty.

🖌 Paint different colours above or below a picture rail or introduce a border two-thirds of the way down the wall (below eyelevel) to add a point of focus that draws the eye down from the ceiling.

Maximize natural light

Choosing the right colour makes an enormous difference to the sense of light and space. Certain shades illuminate dark rooms, while others soften bright light. The key to this is to choose a warm paint tone in rooms with restricted sunshine (small windows or north facing) and a cooler tone in rooms with large windows or plenty of natural light. Warmer tones contain red or yellow pigment, cooler ones contain more blue. This does not mean that blue is always a cold colour – those veering towards turquoise or lilac feel warmer because they contain yellow and/or red pigments.

PICK THE RIGHT PAINT

🖌 Water-based paints for walls and woodwork are easier to use and have a low odour. If your child suffers from allergies or asthma, look for almost odourless paints that are petroleum- and solvent-free.

🖌 For a resilient finish on walls, look for paint with a glossy rather than matt finish – often called vinyl soft sheen – as this is more resistant to grubby finger and crayon marks and can be wiped clean with a damp cloth.

🖌 Oil-based paints are the traditional choice for woodwork and offer a long-lasting and durable finish that resists knocks and is easy to wash. Preparation takes longer as surfaces need sanding and priming carefully. The smell of paint can last for several days afterwards.

🖌 If you want to use the same paint on a variety of areas, choose multi-surface paint for best results. Follow the manufacturer's instructions carefully, and prepare all areas before painting by sanding and washing with detergent.

Mixing colours

Maximum impact or tasteful harmony – the key is found on a colour wheel. The colour wheel on the opposite page shows you what shades work together. Paint manufacturers also produce colour wheels and charts that give a visual guide to which shades enhance each other. Here are three colour-scheming techniques that will give you a scheme that is guaranteed to work.

Monotone these are schemes where you pick colours from the same segment of the colour wheel, so it could be a scheme in toning yellows, blues or green, for example. It is a fail-safe way to choose a palette that works and is also a useful way to tone things down if your child insists that nothing but pink or red will do.

Contrasting these are shades from the opposite side of the wheel, for instance blue and yellow. It is a more daring look, but can be bold and stimulating in a child's room. If you want a subtler effect, go for an almost-opposite – one segment left or right of the opposite colour. Blue and yellow is a classic, almost-opposite pairing.

Harmonious these are chosen from the adjoining colour segment. Classic pairings include green and yellow. The overall effect can be bright or muted depending on the intensity of the colours, but it is invariably cheerful and easy to live with.

◀ *Harmonious: Pick adjoining shades on the colour wheel to create cheerful effects.*

◀ *Contrasting: Combine almost-opposites like yellow and blue for a bold look that is not overpowering.*

▶ *Monotone: Use varying shades of one colour for a restful scheme that is easy to accessorize.*

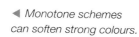

◀ *Monotone schemes can soften strong colours.*

▶ *Harmonious pairings are easy on the eye.*

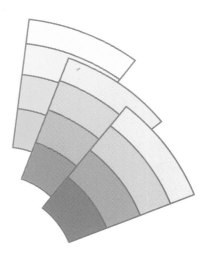

▼ *Contrasting shades create bold effects.*

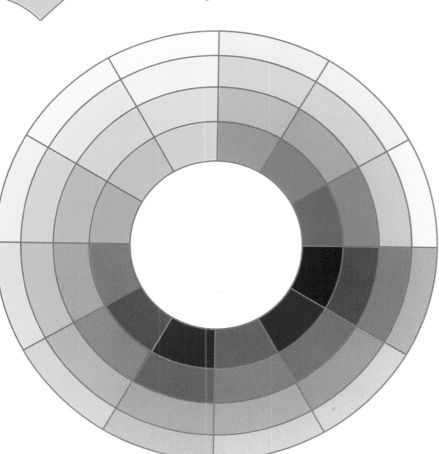

TOP TIPS FOR PICKING PATTERNS

Children love patterns as much as colour and this is an easy way to introduce themes or to satisfy their latest craze for ponies or spaceships. Here are guidelines for choosing and mixing designs:

✎ Match your pattern to the scale of the room. A really large wall or window area can take a bold design, but smaller rooms/areas should have more diminutive designs.

✎ Some patterns work almost anywhere – small spots, stripes and checks add interest without being overwhelming. They are also easy to accessorize and do not date as quickly as some floral or figurative designs.

✎ Don't be afraid to mix patterns. For instance, a bold flower print works well alongside a check provided you ensure at least one colour in the two designs is the same.

✎ Introduce pale elements to tone down bold patterns. This could mean choosing a paper or fabric with a white background, or ensuring that a dark, patterned wallpaper is relieved with areas of pale flooring and plenty of white woodwork.

✎ Let the manufacturers do the hard work for you. Most design companies produce ready-coordinated lines, allowing you to mix and match, secure in the knowledge that the patterns are designed for each other.

WALLPAPER FEATURE WALLS

Papering just one wall is a fashionable and economical way to introduce pattern into an otherwise plain scheme. Not only will you find it easier to do (papering around corners is very tricky), but it also creates a focal point. Use it in small rooms to stop them looking 'boxy', and, in large or high-ceilinged rooms, combine a bold pattern with paint or a plain wallpaper as a means of breaking up the wall space. Make sure the pattern you choose is complemented by the other three walls – the easiest way to do this is to pick out a shade in the wallpaper design and then match this to your paint or paper.

◄ *Papering one wall in a bold pattern is an effective way of breaking up a large area. Here, a co-ordinating border around the room pulls the scheme together.*

Easy special effects

One of the easiest ways to create an individual setting is to introduce special effects in your child's room. You can use stencils as wall art, create a simple border or random pattern with stamps, or introduce a favourite character into the bedroom using border paper or stickers. All these effects are quick and economical, making it easy to introduce change when your child tires of fairies or spaceships. If you want to create your own custom-made effect, try hand-painting stripes. They are quick to do and are an effective way of enlivening a dull wall or updating an existing scheme without a total redecoration.

Stencils

The contemporary way to use stencils is to go for larger designs applied in moderation. Instead of covering all four walls with stencils, choose a bold, simple design and use it sparingly. Unless you are creating a more formal stencilled border, placing should be random rather than orderly – think of this as wall art rather than an all-over decorating technique. You can buy stencils from home improvement stores or stencil specialists. Alternatively, make your own. You can make a template using almost any design, although simple shapes are easiest to do. Choose your shape from a fabric or wallpaper pattern or look for inspiration in children's story books – all you need is an object that can be traced. Instructions for creating your own stencil are opposite and you will also find a selection of simple designs to trace and use as the basis for your own wall art on pages 122–123.

▲ Smaller stencil designs are effective for creating borders or decorating furniture.

◀ Use stencils as wall art – this cat design looks effective over a large wall area.

make your own stencil

To save time, if you are stencilling a large area, make more than one stencil.

YOU WILL NEED

Shape for tracing

Tracing paper

Soft pencil

Strong card or acetate

Scissors or craft knife

Low-tack masking tape

Stencil paints or sticks, or acrylic paint

1 Place a sheet of tracing paper over your chosen pattern and trace around it with a soft pencil.

2 Transfer the design onto a sheet of strong card or acetate (available from art shops). If you want the stencil larger or smaller, transfer the design onto plain paper first, then enlarge or reduce it using a photocopier.

3 Leaving a generous border around the shape so that it is easy to handle, cut away the inside of the design with sharp scissors or a craft knife, ensuring your work surface is protected with newspaper or a craft board before you begin cutting. Discard the cut-out centre, and your stencil is ready for use.

4 Position the stencil on the wall and attach it with a piece of low-tack masking tape on each corner. Use specialist acrylic-based stencil paint or stencil sticks (similar to crayons) to fill in the design. Ordinary acrylic paint also works well. When the design is complete, carefully remove the stencil template from the wall.

▲ These simple motifs can be enlarged on a photocopier to create a larger stencil design.

stripes and checks

Painting your own stripe effects is easy and you can use them to create borders, frame a window or door, or add interest to a dull corner. Once the paint is dry, add stickers, stamp motifs or paint a row of dots on top. Here is the basic method.

YOU WILL NEED

Ruler

Soft pencil

Spirit level or plumb line

Small and large paint pads or rollers

Vinyl matt emulsion (latex)

1 Using a ruler and pencil, mark out the top and bottom edges of the area to be painted. To ensure accuracy, use a spirit level (or a plumb line if the stripe is vertical).

2 Use a small paint pad to create a clean edge for the top and bottom (or either side) of the stripes. Use a larger paint pad to infill the middle of the stripe.

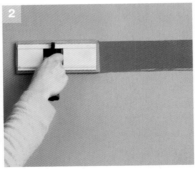

GINGHAM BORDER For a lighter look, paint a folk art-style gingham border. Dilute the paint with a little water first (roughly one-part water to five-parts paint). Mark pencil guidelines, then paint the vertical stripes using a small paint roller. Once they are dry, paint horizontal stripes over the top. Where the roller crosses the vertical stripe, the colour will be darker, just like a gingham check. If you need to reload your roller with paint midway along, stop the roller just inside a vertical line.

▲ *Stamps can be used to create borders or random wallpaper effects. Combine two or three colours for a bolder finish.*

Stamps

Stamps are easy to use and make a great alternative to stencils or wallpaper. Match your stamp to the location – a larger design will look better on a large wall area whereas a small design is suitable for borders or creating details on furniture. Use a stamp paint as it is quick-drying, comes in intense colours, and is ready mixed to the right consistency. You can find special inks for using on fabric if you want to continue a motif onto curtains or cushions. Most inks are permanent, even if the fabric is machine-washed but check the manufacturer's instructions to make sure this is the case. Bear in mind that most stamp paints and inks are not suitable for glossy and shiny surfaces, so if you want to stamp onto an area of woodwork or furniture, paint it first with water-based paint.

Borders

The best thing about borders is that they take minutes to put up and can revitalize a room. There is a huge variety of options, from traditional wallpaper borders to sticky-backed versions. You can also find square or round adhesive motifs that can be lined up to create a border effect.

First, ensure the walls are clean and free from dust and grease. Mark a guideline in pencil or chalk on the wall so that the border will be straight. The easiest way to do this is to make pencil marks at regular intervals along the wall using a long ruler or length of wood.

Measure from the skirting (baseboard) or floor and use the ruler or wood and pencil to create a horizontal guideline. You do not have to place the border halfway down the wall – in smaller rooms it may look more effective closer to the floor. Bear in mind that your child will be able to see and enjoy the pattern more if it is at their eye-level, or below.

▼ *Use border paper or stickers to define the area around a bed. Here, the fairy motif was continued onto the furniture and coat hooks.*

Easy window treatments

There is one golden rule for window treatments in children's rooms – be practical. If allergies are an issue, windows will be easier to clean and keep dust-free if you choose a plain roller blind or a Roman blind. Combine this with tab-top curtains or a fabric panel if you want a dressier effect.

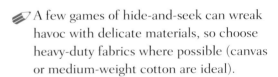 Choose easy-care fabric – preferably one you can wash. If you are making your own curtains, remember to check that all fabrics, linings and trims are compatible when it comes to washing or dry cleaning.

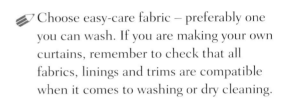 A few games of hide-and-seek can wreak havoc with delicate materials, so choose heavy-duty fabrics where possible (canvas or medium-weight cotton are ideal).

For younger children, your key concern is excluding light, so install a blackout blind or have a dark lining fitted to curtains.

Look for plain, ready-made curtains and customize them by adding colourful tiebacks or sewing on ribbons or patches of bright fabric (see Toy store on pages 26–7).

Ensure curtains and blinds are fixed securely enough to withstand a good tug from your child. Check that curtain and blind cords do not hang down (wind around a sturdy hook midway up the window frame to keep them out of reach).

▲ ▶ *A bold curtain design can be the starting point of your room scheme.*

◀ *In younger children's rooms, choose easy care fabrics that can stand up to their games.*

DESIGN YOUR OWN BLIND

Plain white roller cotton blinds are inexpensive to buy and can be customized to match your room scheme. Here, we added a simple ribbon trim to pick out other colours in the room and create a smart setting for an older child.

In younger children's rooms you can go for fun effects if you decorate a plain blind freehand using fabric markers or felt tips. Pick a simple design that works with your overall scheme and practise on card or paper first. Naïve flowers and animals or simple lettering look particularly effective.

This simple blind is quick and easy to make and because it fits neatly inside the window recess, it is perfect for ensuring a restful night's sleep on light summer evenings. It is also economical with fabric and can be teamed with simple tab-top curtains in neutral or co-ordinating colours to create a formal frame for the window. The fixings are simple eyelets, positioned around the blind so you can set it at different heights.

lights out

1 Measure the window and add 5 cm (2 in) to each side for the seam. This is the amount of fabric you will need to buy.

2 Cut out the fabric, hem all sides and press with an iron.

3 Fix the eyelet poppers evenly along all four fabric edges, following the manufacturer's instructions.

4 Mark the position of the eyelets within the window frame with a pencil. Fix nails or screws inside the top edge of the window frame ensuring you match the spacing to the position of the eyelets.

5 Using the top line of eyelets, hang the blind from the nails or screws. Lift the blind by hooking a lower set of eyelets onto the nails or screws.

USING RIBBON OR CORD With its robust eyelets, this blind is perfect for a nautical-themed bedroom, but you could create a more colourful effect by using strong ribbon or rope cord to hang the blind instead. You will need to stitch it firmly to the blind using a sewing machine. You can also decorate the fabric with appliqué shapes. Iron-on patches for mending children's jeans are easy to add to the blind before you hang it – look for designs with flowers, boats or spaceships and remember that they will look most effective if they are placed along the top or bottom edges so they can be seen when the blind is raised.

Simple patchwork pockets turn plain ready-made curtains into a decorative display area for small toys. If you like, you can make the curtains from scratch using a length of plain cotton and adding simple tab-top fixings. Look for colourful fabric remnants – pattern mixing works well here – and consider continuing the patchwork effect onto cushions or even creating a set of pretty patchwork framed pictures for the walls.

toy store

YOU WILL NEED

Fabric remnants

Ready-made plain cotton curtains

Tape measure

Soft pencil

Scissors

Dressmaker's pins

Cotton thread

1 Start by making the pockets. Cut rectangles from the fabric remnants 1 cm (½ in) larger than you need. You can vary the size and pattern of the remnants to add interest.

2 Snip across the corners of each rectangle, 1 cm (½ in) from each corner for the hem. Using an iron, press a 1 cm (½ in) hem on two long sides and one short side of the rectangle.

3 Fold the remaining short side to create a 1-cm (½-in) hem, then fold a further 1 cm (½ in) to create the top of the pocket. Stitch the top of the pocket.

4 Lay the curtains on a flat surface. Pin, then stitch the pockets into place (a sewing machine will create a neater and stronger finish), leaving the top of the pockets open.

CHOOSING FABRIC Mix and match your fabrics for the best effect, but ensure the pocket fabric is of uniform weight – and preferably lighter than the curtains or the pockets may sag. Remember that the pockets are not designed to hold heavy toys.

USING VOILE If you prefer to use a stronger coloured or patterned fabric for the curtains, try combining it with pockets made of sheer cotton voile. You can also attach ribbons or fabric trims to the tops of the pockets.

A restful zone for sleep

Just like adults, children need to wind down at the end of the day. If the room is a hothouse of primary colours and stimulating patterns, you may find your child will stay awake for too long. You can do a lot to help by establishing a clear bedtime routine, but ensuring the area around the bed is a soft and restful environment will also help achieve restful nights for everyone.

Consider painting or papering the wall around the bed in different colours to create a clear divide between active and sleep areas. If there is room, create a divide between the bed and play areas using a screen or chest of drawers.

Minimize clutter around the bed area. Your child will find it easier to sleep if this is an ordered environment and it will enable him or her to get in and out of bed safely in the night.

Turn the ceiling above the bed into a restful feature. Babies love mobiles, while older children will enjoy staring at a pattern of glow-in-the-dark stars.

A dimmer switch installed on the main overhead lamp is useful to create restful lighting while the child gets ready for bed. It is also useful if your child likes to sleep with a light on. A small reading lamp by the bed will add to a sense of security and help you read a bedtime story.

◀ *A voile canopy adds a sense of security as well as a light and airy feel.*

Use soft, tactile textures around the bed. A canopy over the bed is easy to fit (see page 96) and the sense of enclosure adds a feeling of security. A cosy rug next to the bed and a fleecy throw on top of the duvet are good ways of introducing bedtime comfort. Bear in mind that babies aged under one year need light, cotton bed linen to ensure they do not get too hot.

Ensure there is adequate ventilation to make the room comfortable for sleep. Choosing bed linen in natural materials will help to keep your child cool.

Make sure the bed is comfortable and large enough, with a firm mattress (see Choosing a bed, page 40).

Is noise an issue? If the room overlooks a busy street, additional soundproofing may help. Curtains or blinds with padded linings will also reduce noise. Ensure windows are sealed properly.

Position the TV or computer at least an arm's-length away from the bed. Keep a few favourite toys and books close at hand.

▼ *The area around your child's bed should include soft textures and favourite toys.*

CHAPTER 2

layout, furniture and flooring

Give them space to grow with furniture and fittings that are practical, adaptable and fun

Planning the layout

Children's rooms double up as play and sleep zones. While your main concern is space for clothes and toys, your child wants room for adventure. Even if the area is small or shaped awkwardly, if you plan the layout with care you can create a room that not only feels more spacious, but is also easier to keep tidy. Furniture and flooring get rough treatment from young children's games, so bear in mind wear and tear and choose items that are sturdy and built well. The more floor space you leave, the more likely it is that your child will set up games in the bedroom, rather than commandeering the kitchen or living room floor.

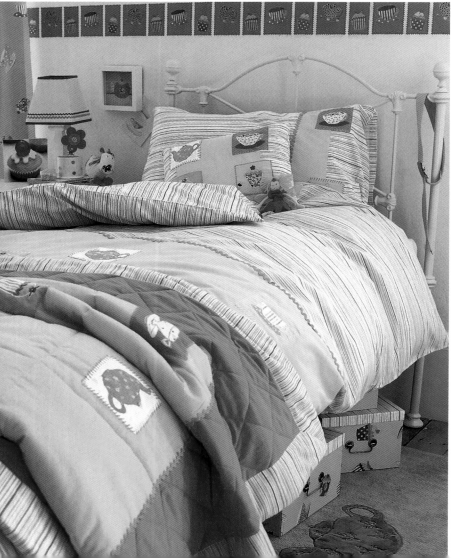

Get the room layout right

Bedrooms are not generally the best spaces to work with. In older homes, they can often be narrow or have sloping ceilings, while in more modern properties they are often small. Start by placing the essentials and then you can add in additional details that make the room feel comfortable as well as practical. Bear in mind that the more floor area you see, the larger the room will appear, so it's worth looking for space-making extras such as wall-hung shelves. Here are more tricks for positioning furniture to suit the shape of your child's room.

▲ *A day bed works well in narrow rooms as it converts from a comfy sofa to a sleeping zone.*

◄ *Pale colours add to a sense of space, so choose a bedstead in a soft shade. Add co-ordinated under-bed storage for toys and games.*

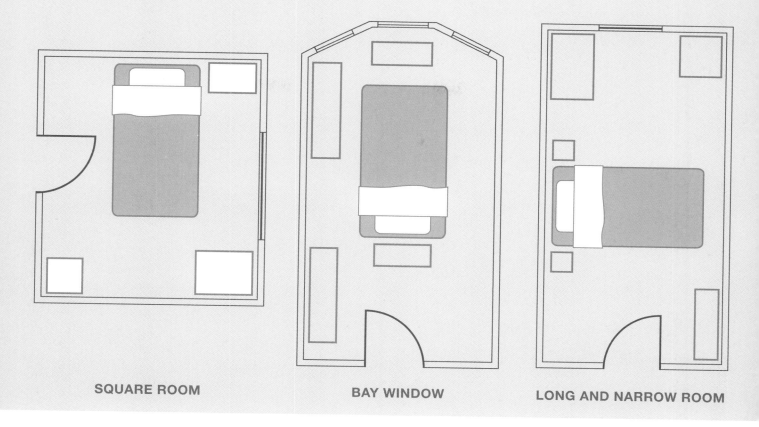

SQUARE ROOM **BAY WINDOW** **LONG AND NARROW ROOM**

Square room

This is the easiest shape to design, but if the room is small, it may feel boxy or confined. The key is to position the bed so you don't bump into it as soon as you open the door. Try moving it away from the entrance – it may help if you rehang the door so it opens the other way. To add interest to the room, face the bed towards a focal point, such as a window, fireplace or a feature wall that you have created using bold paint, wallpaper or colourful pictures.

Bedroom with bay window

This is a classic feature in many older homes and it creates a natural focal point for the room. Position the bed as in a square or rectangular layout (see above), and leave the bay free. The bay makes a great place for a window seat with toy storage underneath, or a neat entertainment zone if you add a table and chairs or a scaled-down sofa. If space is tight and you need to position the bed in the bay, make sure you invest in blackout blinds so your child is not disturbed by light.

Long and narrow room

With two long walls and two short ones, the main problem is where to position the bed. If you site it down one of the long walls, it will emphasize the room's narrow dimensions. Ideally, place it parallel with one of the shorter walls (but away from the wall if possible). If that doesn't work, place it lengthways so the footboard faces towards the door, then add a chest of drawers, toy box, or other low item of furniture at the end so you see that rather than the bed end when you open the door.

If you have to place the bed against a wall because the room is too small for it to work any other way, dress it up by placing cushions where the bed meets the wall – that way the bed feels more like a sofa and becomes a good place for children to read or entertain friends. You could fix a padded board (MDF (composite board) covered with fabric is ideal) along the back wall to act as a sofa back, or invest in a day bed.

Focus on lighting

Bedrooms need a mix of ambient and task lighting, so combine an overhead light fitting or recessed spotlights with side lights for reading and study. One trick used by lighting designers is to 'layer' light by placing fittings at different heights around the room. For example, place lights under a bookcase shelf or fixed to the wall to create softer light-and-shade effects. This also helps to make small or low-ceilinged rooms feel more spacious. Changing bulbs can also improve the atmosphere and complement your colour scheme. Standard tungsten bulbs cast a yellowish light, while tungsten halogen bulbs have a blue aura that is closer to daylight.

◀ *Introduce table lamps to increase the comfort level and provide focused light for reading.*

▶ *At night-time, leave a low light on by your child's cot (crib) or bed if they prefer to sleep with the light on.*

SAFETY FIRST

The best way to ensure you create a safe environment for young children is to imagine yourself at their height. Remember how curious children are and then consider which parts of the room are going to be investigated. Start with things at eye level. What looks enticing to tug off the wall or to climb up? You can't guard against every eventuality, but here are some watch points:

✎ Ensure nursery furniture complies with current fire safety and childcare advice. The same goes for mattresses and bedding. Cots need to comply with specific safety regulations, so check with your retailer before you buy. In particular, there should be no gaps between cot rungs where your child's head, fingers, arms or legs could become trapped.

✎ Sharp angles and corners on furniture may be at head-height for your child and are dangerous if they tumble or run into them. Shield corners with rubber corner covers.

✎ Check that the furniture is stable when doors or drawers are opened. Also check that hinges can't trap fingers.

✎ Trunks make useful toy storage, but avoid designs with heavy lids that could fall on your child's head or neck.

✎ Steer clear of furniture or fittings that might shatter. Glass lampshades, mirrors and other easy-to-break objects are best kept well away from children's rooms. Door panes *must* be in safety glass.

✎ Attach pictures and shelves to the wall with particular care. Try the tug test – if you can pull something off the wall, so might your child.

✎ If your child is very young, install window locks or bars on windows that could be opened. Make sure there is no internal lock on the bedroom door.

✎ In young children's rooms, fit protective covers over electrical sockets to stop fingers getting stuck into them. Also ensure there are no hanging electrical wires – if they are visible, anchor them to the wall with cable pins.

✎ Rugs should be fixed to the floor with adhesive grippers to stop them becoming a trip hazard.

These simple lampshade projects are a quick way to dress up a child's bedroom. Add colourful ribbons to jazz up a plain white lampshade or go for fun effects with bold white spots and a bobble trim. Choose colours to match your room scheme – or pick a bold contrast to turn a lamp into a feature.

seeing spots

YOU WILL NEED

Newspaper

Lampshade

Spray paint

Stationery stickers

Superglue

Bobble trim

1 Work in a well-ventilated area. Use newspaper to cover the surrounding area, and then spray paint the lampshade. Move the can from left to right and work steadily. You may find it easier to spray the lampshade in stages and leave it to dry between coats.

2 Once the lampshade is covered evenly with paint, stick on your dots working around the shade from top to bottom.

3 Dab superglue onto the bottom rim of the shade and attach the bobble trim in place. Leave to dry thoroughly before you put the shade back on the lamp.

ribbon shade

YOU WILL NEED

Plain white lampshade

Pencil

Tape measure

Variety of colourful ribbon

Scissors

Velcro pads or PVA glue

1 Make small pencil marks at regular intervals down the lampshade. Use a tape measure to position them accurately.

2 Cut the ribbons to the circumference of the lampshade (add on a small overlap which you can trim later), and work around the lampshade using self-adhesive Velcro pads or PVA glue. If you use glue, wipe off any excess as you work or it will show through when the bulb is on.

INSTANT TRIMS: This instant trim method is so effective you may find it becomes addictive. Why not attach a simple trim to a duvet or cushion cover as well? You may prefer to stitch the trim with a sewing machine if the item is to be washed.

Choose the right furniture

A wardrobe bought for clothes is just as likely to become a hiding place, while the table you chose so carefully could become a climbing frame. Bearing this in mind, choose furniture and fittings based on three key criteria: robustness, durability and ease of use.

✏ Is it robust? If the furniture wobbles when you touch it, this is something that may not survive children's games. Large items, such as wardrobes and chests of drawers should stand firm – even with doors and drawers open – so that there is no risk of toppling over.

✏ Will it last? Look for items that can adapt as your child grows. Can it be repainted and still look good when the room is redecorated?

✏ Is the furniture easy to use? Adult-sized wardrobes and drawers can be hard to reach and open. Children will be encouraged to tidy up for themselves and become independent if they have easy access to their own clothes and toys.

Built-in storage

In cramped or awkward shaped rooms – particularly those with angled ceilings or corners – built-in wardrobes/closets are the most practical design solution for maximizing storage. The materials and labour costs for a built-in wardrobe/closet may seem on the high side, but this investment could transform a dead zone into floor-to-ceiling storage. For children's rooms choose cheaper materials, such as plain MDF (composite board), and then paint the cupboard with water- or oil-based wood paint. An MDF cupboard will need a coat of primer and two to three topcoats to ensure a smart finish.

If you have old or tired fitted cupboards already in place, they could be worth revamping. If you can't find new doors that fit the units (home improvement stores stock a variety of plain and slatted versions) ask a carpenter to design made-to-measure doors to update them. Alternatively, paint the doors and add new door handles for a fresh look. Look at the internal layout – it may be worth altering the configuration of shelves or installing a hanging rail lower down to create more useable storage space.

▲ New handles update old furniture in an instant.

MAKE FITTED FURNITURE A FEATURE

Fitted furniture can easily dominate a room, so it's a good idea to choose your colour scheme with care. Often, a matching or toning shade of paint will make the cupboard look less obtrusive – particularly if you choose a soft and subtle version of your wall colour. Break up the effect by adding motifs on the doors. These can be stencilled or stamped, or you can stick on cut-out wallpaper shapes.

◄ *Update existing fitted cupboards/closets with bright paint and new handles.*

Choosing a bed

A solid bed with a firm mattress is just as important for children as it is for adults, so this is the most important investment you can make for your child's bedroom. Bearing in mind that children under seven need up to 12 hours sleep a night, it is worth choosing one that not only provides adequate back support, but is long and wide enough to be really comfortable. Here are key guidelines:

▶ *Look for designs that they won't outgrow.*

▼ *If you choose a bedstead, ensure it has space underneath for storage.*

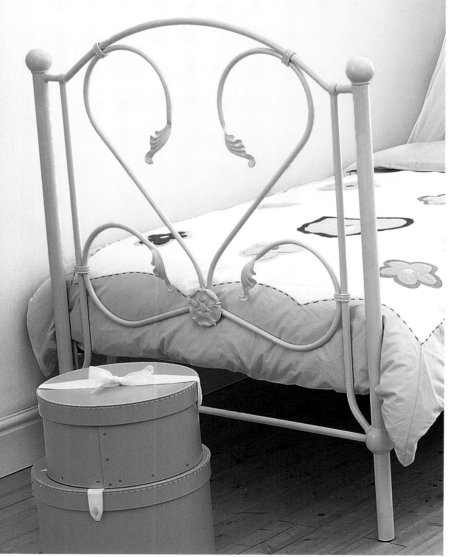

🛏 Look for a good quality foam or sprung mattress that offers back support. If it is a new mattress for an existing bed frame, make sure the two are compatible. Check that the mattress carries an appropriate fire safety label.

🛏 The bed frame should not wobble. If it is self-assembly, check that the fittings are robust without sharp edges and are too firm to be unscrewed without proper tools.

🛏 The average size for a child's bed is 75 cm (2 ft 6 in) or 90 cm (3 ft) wide. Choose the wider size if you can, and check the bed is long enough. Consider an extendable bed with a fold-down head- and footboard to accommodate the next growth spurt.

🛏 Look for a design that offers extra storage. Divans often have storage drawers underneath and if you choose a traditional bedstead, look for one that has enough clearance to place storage boxes below it. For the ultimate in storage, choose a cabin bed, which sits on a raised platform and offers capacious cupboard or play space underneath (see opposite). This style of bed is not generally recommended for very young children.

CABIN AND BUNK BEDS

Raised beds are great spacesavers. If you choose a cabin design, it offers capacious storage underneath. Some designs have an area underneath where you can stow a desk, or unfold a second bed when your child has friends to stay. If you have two children sharing a room, a bunk makes a practical option.

Raised beds can diminish a room's sense of light – particularly if ceilings are low or angled – so look for a design in slatted light wood or metal. Also incorporate the bed into the design of the room. For example, buy a nautical duvet cover and hang blue and white pennants from the bed frame, and that oversized design has become a smart sailing rig.

Raised beds should have guard rails and the top of the mattress should sit at least 10 cm (4 in) below the top of the rail so your child can't fall out of bed. Check that the gaps between slats are no more than 7.5 cm (3 in) wide and the ladder is fixed to the bed. The ladder's treads should be at least 30 cm (12 in) wide and 20 cm (8 in) apart.

With bunks, check that there is enough clearance for the child on the bottom to sit up without banging his or her head. Make sure that the top bunk is a safe distance from the ceiling. A raised bed is not recommended for children under six.

This easy project is a great way to add interest to a plain wardrobe and can be used to revamp an old piece of furniture so that it fits into your child's room. Borrow motifs from soft furnishings or wallpaper to tie the wardrobe into the bedroom scheme. We chose classic hearts and flowers, but spaceships, boats or animals could work just as well. Simple designs look most effective and are easy to cut out neatly.

cupboard love

YOU WILL NEED

Tracing paper

Soft pencil

Scissors or craft knife

Patterned sticky-backed plastic

1 Place a sheet of tracing paper over your chosen shape (here we chose a heart) and draw around the outline of the shape with a pencil. Cut out the shape to make a template. If you decide on a small image as the basis of your wardrobe design – for instance from wallpaper – enlarge it on a photocopier before you trace it so that the finished motif has more impact.

2 Place the template on the patterned sticky-back plastic, trace around it and cut it out carefully using sharp scissors. You can use a craft knife if you prefer a cleaner edge, but remember to rest the plastic on a board or pile of newspapers so that you don't damage your work surface.

3 Position the heart shape on the wardrobe. When you're happy with the position, peel off the backing and press it firmly into place. Cut out the rest of the shapes in the same way and position them randomly around the doors.

TIP: To create a balanced design, cut out all the shapes first and position roughly before peeling off the plastic backing. Mark the spot for each motif using a soft pencil. Mixing different sizes and shapes creates a more informal look.

ALTERNATIVE: Cut motifs straight from wallpaper and stick them onto the wardrobe door with glue or wallpaper paste. They will fade or curl over time, so apply a coat of clear varnish over the door afterwards for longevity.

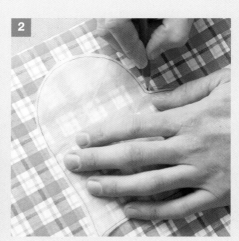

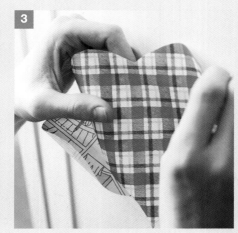

This technique works best on a white- or pastel-painted wardrobe. Pine or oak wardrobes are easy to paint provided you prepare them properly. Sand to remove all varnish, wash with sugar soap or detergent, prime with wood undercoat, and then apply two coats of wood or multi-surface paint (water or acrylic-based paint is low-odour and easier to apply). If you prefer, use a white or cream wood stain instead. It is even quicker to apply and will give the wardrobe a rustic effect.

This project is a simple way to add interest to a plain wardrobe, especially if you use leftover wallpaper so that it matches the room décor. Lower the hanging rail and add extra shelves at the same time to improve the storage inside.

animal crackers

YOU WILL NEED

Tape measure

Wallpaper

Scissors

Wallpaper paste

Craft knife

Animal stickers or motifs from wallpaper offcuts

1 Remove existing shelves or hanging rails. Measure the back wall of the wardrobe and cut your wallpaper to size. You may find it easier to leave a 2.5-cm (1-in) border all round and then trim the wallpaper with a Stanley knife once it is pasted into position.

2 Ensure the back of the wardrobe is clean and dust-free. Apply a layer of wallpaper paste and glue the wallpaper carefully into position. Trim the edges where necessary.

3 Replace the shelves and hanging rail when the wallpaper is fully dry (allow at least eight hours). Finish by decorating the back of the wardrobe doors with motifs cut from wallpaper offcuts, or use stickers.

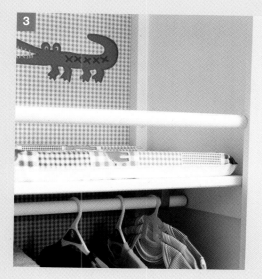

TIPS: Choose a simple pattern – a check is ideal – so you do not have to align the pattern too carefully. You could use sticky-backed plastic instead of wallpaper.

If the back of the wardrobe is uneven, cut a piece of cardboard or thin plywood to size, attach the wallpaper onto that, and then fix the board to the back of the wardrobe with glue or a staple gun.

If you want to add a new internal shelf, measure the width and depth of your wardrobe and get a timber merchant (lumberyard) to cut a piece of 2 cm (approx ¾ in) MDF (composite board) to size. Paint the MDF with oil-based paint such as satinwood. You'll need to firmly glue and screw lengths of 2 x 2 cm (¾ x ¾ in) wooden battens to the wardrobe sides to support the shelves (drill from the outside of the wardrobe). Ask a timber merchant to cut the battens to size for you. You could also add a half-depth shelf above for extra storage, and a length of 3·cm (approx 1¼ in) dowelling for a hanging rail.

Brighten a plain chest of drawers by designing your own drawer-front motif. We created a tan cowhide design that is perfect for a Wild West-themed bedroom, but it's easy to find a design to fit your room scheme – consider flowers, stars or seashells. Get inspiration from a piece of fabric or wallpaper before you start, as you'll need to draw the outline of your chosen motif onto the drawer fronts.

camouflage treatment

YOU WILL NEED

Screwdriver

Spray paint

Sandpaper

Cloth

Pencil

Emulsion (latex) paint

Fine paintbrush

Clear matt varnish

1 Pull out the drawers and remove the drawer handles with a screwdriver. Lay the handles onto newspaper and decorate with spray paint – we used chrome. Set aside to dry.

2 Sand the drawer fronts lightly to create a keyed surface for the paint. Wipe with a damp cloth to remove the dust.

3 Plan your drawer front design using your chosen fabric or wallpaper as a reference point. You may find you can draw the outline onto the drawers freehand using a soft pencil. Alternatively, trace the outline and use a piece of card as your template.

4 Fill in the outline using the emulsion paint and a fine paintbrush. Set aside to dry and add a second coat if necessary. Apply two coats of clear matt varnish to protect the design.

TIP: You may prefer to change the drawer handles rather than spray-painting them. You could start with new drawer handles and design your motif around them. For instance, a bright yellow drawer handle could become the centrepiece for a colourful flower design.

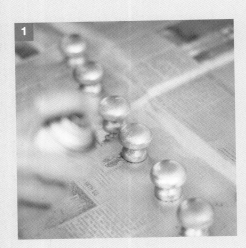

DECORATOR'S NOTE:

If you need to paint the chest of drawers before you add your design, sand first using a coarse-grade sandpaper. Prime with undercoat or water-based primer, then apply two coats of multi-surface emulsion (latex).

Childproof flooring

Flooring has to be chosen with care. You want it to look good, be easy to clean, and resilient to spills and knocks. But even more than that, it has to last, so look for designs neither you nor your child will tire of and make sure it's tough enough to withstand children's games. Always check before you buy that the flooring is specifically recommended for children's rooms. Here are the options.

Carpet

A soft and cushioning surface, carpet is also good at reducing noise (useful for those sitting downstairs). It's also safe if your child takes a tumble. Choose cut rather than looped pile as it is softer and easier to maintain. A wool mix is worth the investment (80–20 wool–man-made is a good choice) because it will look good for longer. The budget option is polypropylene, but although it is ultra-durable, the pile becomes flattened, so it doesn't maintain its appearance over time. Another option is to buy contract carpet designed for offices – usually it has a robust cord finish and although it's not particularly soft underfoot it does stand up to heavy wear and tear. Do buy a good underlay as this will extend the life of your carpet considerably and help with reducing noise. With all carpet, vacuum regularly, and have it cleaned professionally if there has been a major spill.

▲ Natural flooring adds a contemporary finish.

◄ Carpet is soft and comfortable underfoot and good at deadening noise.

Natural flooring

This tends to be more difficult to clean than carpet, but it does have a tough finish and a contemporary look. Seagrass is the smoothest and flattest of the weaves. It's hardwearing and stain-resistant, but can be slippery underfoot. Sisal is tougher still and comes in a wide variety of shades. Choose one with a stain protective finish and consider a sisal/wool blend for extra comfort. Avoid coir and jute; coir is too prickly to go barefoot in comfort, and jute is not durable enough to stand up to spills and rough play.

Laminate

Available in a variety of shades from bleached pine to dark wood effects, laminate floors are easy to lay yourself. The surface can be slippery so if you add a rug, make sure it is anchored securely with adhesive rug-fixing strips. Bear in mind that some laminates may become dented if sharp or heavy objects are dropped onto them (check with your retailer before you buy). Maintenance is straightforward – regular vacuuming or brushing to remove dust and a mopping once or twice a week. Spills should be wiped up as soon as possible.

Wooden boards

If you are lucky enough to have original or reclaimed wooden floorboards, then you score highly in the style and maintenance stakes. The floor will need to be sanded and sealed to guard against splinters. Make sure the gaps between boards are sealed with wood filler (wood putty) to stop the floor becoming a dust trap or home for stray pencils and crumbs. If the floorboards aren't in great condition, painting them is a way to introduce colour (see Set square floor, pages 50–1, for decorating inspiration). Wood can be hard on knees and unforgiving when children fall over, so consider adding rugs.

▶ *Wood and laminates are easy to maintain.*

Vinyl

A good, practical choice, vinyl sheet or tile flooring is hardwearing and comes in a vast range of colourways. Add colourful rugs and you have a surface that looks good and can withstand the toughest treatment. You also have a choice of price points, from budget vinyl tiles you lay yourself, to luxury floors that need professional installation. Choose a cushioned surface as this will reduce sound and be more forgiving if your child takes a tumble. Vinyl is easy to sweep or mop clean and generally highly stain-resistant. A ten-year warranty is typical and some are guaranteed for up to 25 years.

WILL IT LAST?

Flooring is one of the most expensive purchases, so avoid anything too bright. A muted shade of beige, grey or blue acts as a neutral backdrop and means you can redecorate without having to match colours. You can brighten the floor by adding colourful rugs that complement the rest of your decorating scheme.

This chequerboard floor is a good way to revive bare wooden floorboards, and children will love playing hopscotch on the giant squares. We chose a soft blue and cream design, but it would work equally well with a stronger contrast such as bold green or pink.

set square floor

YOU WILL NEED

Length of timber

Tape measure

Pencil

Craft knife

Woodwash in two colours

Paintbrush

Artist's paintbrush

Large paintbrush

Clear matt or satin varnish

1 Make sure the floorboards are clean and smooth before you start painting. Fill in any gaps between the boards with wood filler (wood putty). Use the length of timber to create a straight-edge, then mark out a chequerboard pattern using a tape measure and pencil. Score the pencil lines with a Stanley knife to provide a clear guide and to stop the colourwash running into adjacent squares.

2 Apply the lighter woodwash over the whole floor and leave this to dry according to the manufacturer's instructions.

3 Using the artist's brush, paint around the edges of the darker coloured squares. Fill in the squares with the large paintbrush and leave to dry as before. Finish with at least two coats of clear matt or satin varnish.

GOING DOTTY This technique can also be used to create a cheerful rug-effect panel on a wooden floor. We painted the floor yellow with oil-based paint, added a darker green border, and finished off with a pattern of dots painted using the end of a small foam roller.

TIPS: Large squares work best and are quicker to paint, but adapt the square size to suit the room. Start marking out squares from the centre of the room and don't worry if you finish with half- or quarter-squares at the edges – this adds to the chequerboard effect.

For a hardwearing floor, use an oil-based paint such as satinwood. Use one-part paint to one-part white spirit (turpentine) and paint with a large brush. Mark off your surfaces to be painted with masking tape. You'll need to allow a longer drying time between coats.

Radiator covers

It makes practical good sense to cover radiators. Not only does this stop children being burned, getting fingers stuck or dropping crayons into the recess behind, but you also get a useful display shelf and a much smarter finish. MDF (composite board) covers are stocked by home improvement stores in a range of standard radiator sizes, or you could ask a carpenter to construct a simple frame. Ensure the thermostat is still accessible so you can adjust the temperature. For non-standard covers, specialist companies can create just about any design you want, from alphabet letters to circles and hearts.

PAINTING A RADIATOR COVER

Radiator covers are generally supplied in bare MDF ready for you to paint to match your scheme. Paint the radiator with MDF primer first and allow to dry thoroughly (switch the radiator off while you're painting). Paint the cover in satinwood or water-based wood paint. Make sure you get paint on all cut surfaces on the grille area at the front. Apply a second coat of paint and leave to dry thoroughly before you turn the radiator back on.

▲ *This alphabet design is perfect for a nursery.*

◄ *Cut-out circles turn a radiator into a smart focal point.*

► *Match your radiator cover to your wall paint for an understated look.*

Creative space for play

It can be tempting to over-fill your child's room with furniture, particularly if you have lots of toys and clothes to accommodate, but it is far better to be selective and choose pieces that earn their keep. The larger the floor space you can leave free, the more your child will spread out and enjoy creative play. Chapter 3 (pages 56–79) focuses on storage solutions that will help you organize clothes and toys, but here are some guidelines to help you make the best use of space and provide plenty of room for fun and games.

- Create more floor space by choosing dual-purpose pieces such as tables with storage space underneath or seats that convert into beds (useful for sleep-over parties).

- Lightweight and portable, beanbags and stackable or folding chairs are useful and can be moved without your help. Check the weight before you buy.

- Find room for a desk or table where you can both sit for drawing, painting or crafts. Add task lighting and a comfortable chair. Later on this area will be used for homework.

- Are there under-utilized areas around the room that can be adapted for storage or seating? A window seat with storage underneath or a small cupboard in the recess next to a chimney breast makes great use of space. For the best use of space, ask a carpenter to construct a cupboard or seat to fit.

- If you are adding a fitted bookshelf or cupboard, consider having it built on legs so that the space at floor level can be utilized as easy-access storage for books, board games or shoes.

- Source furniture that is fun to look at and to use. Consider beach hut-style wardrobes, animal-shaped chairs and bookshelves shaped like upturned boats that can feed an imagination as well as house lots of stuff.

- Use colour to make practical and bulky pieces of furniture more fun. You can mix and match painted and plain pieces – the key thing is to create an environment that is fun to spend time in.

◄ *Store larger toys in wardrobes or set aside a designated area where these can be kept.*

▶ *Introduce bold colour to furniture and wall shelves.*

CHAPTER 3

simple storage and clever details

Transform their room into a proper den with neat storage and personalized accessories

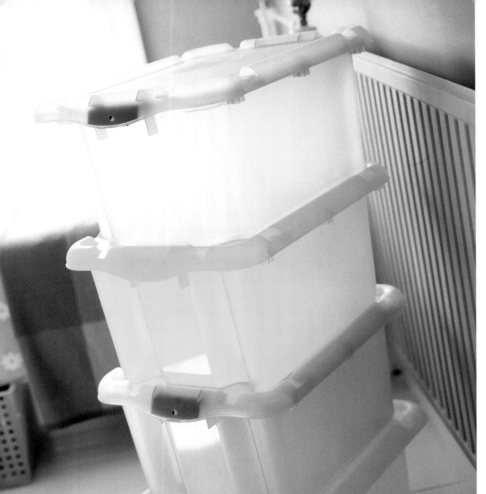

How to choose storage

Before you buy storage you have to consider the needs of your child. If he or she is toddler-age, easily accessible and lightweight crates and boxes are the practical choice for holding toys and games. As your child grows, he or she will need space for books, a computer and homework essentials, so a mix of open shelves, moveable storage and cupboard space is the most practical solution. Here are guidelines to help you include the right elements in your scheme:

✐ Wicker is a classic, inexpensive and durable material that won't date. The most useful buys are lidded laundry baskets (great for dressing up clothes and sports kit), open boxes and mini shelf units.

Get organized!

It is the details that transform your child's bedroom from a functional space into a comfortable setting for imaginative play. Storage is essential – and no one ever claims to have enough, but you have to strike the right balance in children's rooms. Too many deep cupboards and secret hidey-holes and you feed a child's natural tendency to accumulate vast piles of clutter. Too few places to put things and you won't be able to maintain order. You also need to encourage children to tidy up, and the best way to achieve this is to make organisation fun. Go for bright, stackable and moveable pieces – that way you can add variety, as your child's needs change. Add clever personalized details and you will provide a space that truly belongs to your child – and he or she will want to look after it for him or herself.

Plastic boxes are easy to wash – a key concern in nurseries and toddlers' rooms – and come in a range of cheerful colours. You can also buy them in flatpack design so they can be stowed away when they are no longer needed.

Look out for pieces that could be revamped or recycled for the room. Old office filing cupboards make good bedside tables and desk tidy drawers offer neat compartments for stowing art materials, dolls' clothes or farmyard menageries.

Open shelving is invaluable, but it can make a small room feel even more enclosed. Single shelves are a neat alternative – place them around the wall to utilize dead space (above the bed is a good spot) and add colourful bookends to keep things in place.

Peg rails make smart open storage for hanging clothes and coats. Make sure you secure rails firmly to the wall using a drill and plastic wall plugs and position them at a height your child can reach easily.

Is the wardrobe earning its keep? Young children rarely need an adult-sized wardrobe and many clothes can be folded rather than hung. Consider converting most of the wardrobe into shelf space and then fitting a low hanging rail for items that have to be hung up. A hanging rail on wheels may be useful.

Don't forget to utilize hanging space behind the door and inside the wardrobe. Canvas or clear plastic pockets are a useful place for socks and hair accessories. Hang on sturdy hooks and add colourful labels to show what goes where.

Increase storage space and avoid the pre-school hunt for missing items by investing in drawer and wardrobe organisers for stashing easy-to-lose items.

Shop smart

Go shopping in kitchen and bathroom departments – not only are they full of good ideas, but the storage is generally both robust and inexpensive. Lightweight chrome shelf units make great homes for books and computer essentials, while utensil hanging rails are useful on a bedroom wall for hanging belts, jewellery and hair bands. Don't forget to check out the small containers too – clear plastic bathroom jars make a great 'see-at-a-glance' home for small toys and accessories and coloured plastic food containers offer stackable and unbreakable storage space.

▶ *These brightly coloured drawers liven up this otherwise dull storage unit.*

Use the colour code

Children love to discover new things and one of the smartest ways to encourage tidy tendencies when they are very young is to turn tidying up into a learning game. Organize storage by colour – say, soft toys in the yellow drawer and building blocks in the blue – so that your child will memorize the rainbow as they stow things in the right compartment. As your child gets older, introduce pictures, numbers, alphabet letters or whole words. Changing the game as they grow will keep it fresh and your child will continue to learn while you get willing help with the tidying.

Revamp old furniture

It's easy to give a face lift to furniture that has seen better days. Drawer fronts from an old unit make perfect storage containers. Cover them inside and out with colourful wipe-down sticky-back plastic to convert them into slimline and practical underbed storage. The revamped drawers are perfect for stowing away clothes or bed linen and the handles make the drawers easy to retrieve when you need to vacuum the floor or get to the contents.

◀ *These recycled lined drawers make excellent underbed storage units.*

Co-ordinate storage

Small items such as a mini set of drawers can be decorated to coordinate with the walls. Take the drawer fronts out and measure them for size, then cover them with wallpaper offcuts. Unscrew the drawer handles first to make the wallpapering easier.

Simple stowaway panel

Store hairbrushes, socks or other oddments in a simple panel with see-through pockets. Make your own by cutting a panel of fabric to the required size. Choose lightweight transparent fabric, such as voile, for lighter objects, or a sturdier fabric, such as cotton canvas to stow shoes or toys. Add a 1-cm (½-in) seam all round the panel and stitch cord or fabric handles to the top.

◀ This small, wooden six-drawer set gives the room a smart, coordinated look.

▼ See-through pockets mean that oddments are stored away neatly but easy to find.

▼ This cool office-style filing cabinet with its many drawers and cupboards will encourage children to keep their space tidy.

Toy storage

Books, toys and games can turn children's rooms into clutter zones. If you want to keep some sense of order – and make tidying up less of a chore – ensure instantly accessible storage is an integral part of the bedroom design. The following display ideas keep favourite things in view and make tidying up child's play.

Recycle

Brightly-painted tins get a new lease of life as stowaways for small treasures. They even have carry-handles to make tidying up easier and you can hang them from a shelf with cup hooks. Here we used squiggles, stripes and dots to create a toning scheme. Clean out containers thoroughly, ensuring there are no sharp metal edges, before decorating them and use specialist enamel paints to paint the tins.

Bag

Sturdy shopping bags in plastic or wicker are ideal for stashing awkward-shaped toys and are useful for carrying up and down stairs or taking on weekend trips. Look for wide-bottomed bags with robust handles and choose bright colours that match the bedroom scheme.

Pin

Two rows of brightly coloured tacks or wooden pegs can be used to display cards, trophies and artworks. Tacks can be pushed straight into the wall, whereas pegs need to be attached more securely by drilling a hole in the wall, inserting a rawl plug (wall anchor) and screwing in the peg. String ribbon between the two so that objects can be pinned in place. If you don't want to make lots of holes in the wall, hang a pin board or blackboard instead to create a dedicated display zone.

BURIED TREASURE

While old favourites must always be close at hand, children's rooms will be much neater if you rotate their toys by hiding some away. Home improvement stores sell blank pine boxes sturdy enough to hold bears, dolls and building bricks and small enough to put under the bed. Paint or stain the boxes if you want a co-ordinated look – add labels if you like things organised. A cheap alternative is to recycle strong shoe boxes, covering them with bright wrapping paper, wallpaper offcuts or sticky-back plastic. Toy rotation makes your life less cluttered, and it allows children to rediscover long-forgotten dolls or bears and treat them like new. So next time it's raining or they are bored, send them on a treasure hunt in their bedroom!

Hang

Old fashioned laundry bags are simple to make: machine stitch two long sides and one short side of a rectangle, stitch a casing at the open end and thread a cord or length of elasticated string through the casing. Laundry bags can accommodate toys and books as well as clothes. Hang them from the bedstead, wardrobe or door for quick tidy-ups. Look out for oddments of floral, striped or spotted cotton fabric in the sales, or choose sturdy canvas or ticking if you want a bag that's really strong.

Display

Miniature wicker shopping bags suspended on the wall look colourful and make a useful place to store small toys and accessories. Choose bags in the same colour to create a border effect or alternate colours for impact. We placed ours in an orderly row, but they'd look equally effective grouped in a square or circle.

Store

Crayons and felt-tip pens have a habit of getting crushed into the carpet or leaking all over the duvet cover. Encourage children's artistic tendencies by buying an assembly of jewel-coloured plastic tumblers for storing essential craft materials. Jam jars can serve the same purpose and you can add sticky labels so everything goes back into its proper home.

A plain trunk or chest is simple to transform with a coat of paint and colourful motifs. We chose a bold blue and added transport-themed images that are perfect for a car-mad boy or girl, but animals, flowers or nautical images would do just as well. To make your toy chest portable as well as practical, add cord handles and sturdy castors.

box of tricks

YOU WILL NEED

Vinyl matt emulsion (latex)

2 paintbrushes

Wallpaper motifs

Scissors

PVA glue

Clear matt varnish

1 Paint the chest with two coats of vinyl matt emulsion. Leave to dry thoroughly after each coat.

2 Carefully cut around your chosen paper motifs and plan your design on the toy chest – these motifs were placed randomly, but if you are using the same motif throughout, you may want to place it in orderly lines. It will help if you place the objects, then mark each position in pencil before you start gluing.

3 Apply PVA glue to the back of the shapes and stick them to the chest. Set aside to dry following manufacturer's guidelines.

4 Paint the chest with three coats of clear matt varnish, leaving it to dry between each coat.

DECORATOR'S NOTE: *Add castors and handles before you start painting. Drill a hole in the base of each leg and screw in castors. To create cord handles, measure then drill two small holes about 5 cm (2 in) apart on either side of the chest. Thread a length of cord through the holes on one side of the chest and secure both ends inside with knots. Repeat on the other side.*

Fabric panels are an easy way to dress up a functional piece of storage and you can co-ordinate them with your room scheme. We used ours to conceal a wooden storage unit, but they would be just as useful for disguising a cluttered bookshelf or turning an alcove into a neat wardrobe area.

curtain call

YOU WILL NEED

Tape measure

Wooden net rods, for curtain pole

Hacksaw (optional)

Screwdriver

Metal clothes rail

Lightweight fabric, cut and hemmed to size

Fabric pincer clips

1 Measure the area to be covered by the curtains and buy wooden net rods to fit (cut to size using a hacksaw, if required). We used one net rod for the front of the unit and another cut into two pieces for the sides.

2 Fix the rods to the outside of the unit with a screwdriver, positioning them as close as possible to the top of the unit. Fit the clothes rail inside the unit.

3 Attach the fabric panels to the rods using pincer clips. Space at regular intervals along the curtain tops.

DECORATOR'S NOTE:

Choose lightweight fabric so it hangs well and is not too heavy for the net rods – we used a simple, checked voile. To save time on sewing, hem the tops and bottoms of your fabric using an iron-on adhesive hemming tape available from haberdashers (notions counters). For a no-sew alternative, choose ready-made curtains instead.

TIP: If you are curtaining an alcove, choose a strong curtain rail and fix it securely to either side of the alcove using a drill and plastic wall plugs. For extra stability, fix a wooden batten across the alcove first and attach the curtain rail to it.

Focus on details

Once you have decorated the four walls and decided on flooring and storage, the fun really starts. There are no limits on the small details that make this a personal space. Your child will probably have his or her own firm ideas about the colours and decorations they want in the room. There are wonderful accessories to buy, but you can also create customized objects yourself. This is not a setting where you have to worry about minimalism or restraint, so be creative and relish the opportunity to break a few rules.

Try DIY artwork

Every picture tells a story, so buy plain picture and display frames and fill them with DIY artwork. A fragment from a favourite children's book preserved in a hand-painted wooden frame will add to the sense that this is your child's space to decorate and enjoy. You can even create art to order; ask your child to design an image based on the room's colour scheme or his or her latest adventure.

Add personal mementos

Children accumulate a whole host of memories from everyday experiences – be it scout camp or a weekend trip to the beach – and it's important to provide display space for these items. You will have your own ideas about important milestones, be it baby booties or the first painting of you. Set aside shelf space for at least some of these treasures and add pin boards to the wall so that artwork, photos, prizes and other important objects can continue to find a home in the room.

Introduce bright fabrics

This is one of the easiest ways to make a theme work or make changes when your child's tastes change. Look for instant change options such as reversible duvet covers and do not be afraid to mix and match bright colours. Plain, striped, spotted and checked pieces can work with just about any pattern and help to keep the room looking fresh. Look in sales for bargain odd pillowcases and sheets. You could buy plain items and create your own designs.

Focus on the floor

Children spend a lot more time on the floor than adults so make the floor a welcoming place for sprawling to draw or read. Colourful rugs give the room an instant makeover. Look for soft textures and patterns that introduce colour as well as comfort underfoot. Add lightweight and portable seating such as bean-bags and floor cushions.

flower power

Bring the garden into the bedroom by attaching artificial flowers to plain cushion covers. Go for bold colours – we chose cheerful golden yellow gerberas – and continue the theme onto curtains by adding tiebacks braided with flower heads.

YOU WILL NEED

Artificial flowers

Plain cushion

Scissors or craft knife

High-tack adhesive or Velcro

1 Remove the stalks from the flowers with scissors or a craft knife before attaching the flowers to the cushion. Stick the flowers using high-tack adhesive or attach with pieces of Velcro (this allows you to remove the flowers when you want to wash the cushion cover).

NOTE: Parts of the flowers could be a choking hazard, so use only in older children's rooms.

DECORATE WITH TOYS

Some toys are just too magical to be stowed away in the toybox and it is worth creating a special display area where they can be admired – even if your child is still too young to play with them. This is also a good place to include a few heirloom objects – old books and games you played with as a child that bring back happy memories.

Picture perfect

Children love making their own personalized artworks and with a project like this he or she can also decorate a frame to match. The child's initial is stitched onto a square of gingham fabric and then mounted in a pretty painted and flower-decorated frame. This design looks effective on a mantelpiece, but you could even spell out the whole name in a series of frames and then hang them in a line on the wall. For a bold effect that works in a larger frame, create a design in contrasting felts – this would also be easier for younger children to stitch.

Just add hooks

Add a wood or MDF (composite board) panel to the wall and then attach coat hooks to the panel so you can hang up jewellery, hair-ties and school bags. We chose heart-shaped metal hooks that look perfect in an older girl's room, but you could use colourful plastic or animal motif designs or Shaker-style wooden pegs if you prefer. Make sure the panel is positioned securely using a drill, rawl plugs (wall anchors) and screws, and site it in an area of the room where your child won't run into the hooks.

Storage seat

Unpainted wooden chests can be customized easily to create storage with occasional seating on top. Paint the sides of the trunk with two coats of satinwood paint. Measure the lid and cut the fabric to size with a large seam (around 10 cm / 4 in) all round. Position the fabric on the trunk lid and fix it in place with a staple gun to the underside of the lid. For a neat finish, fold the material over on itself or cover the underside with a rectangle of plain lining fabric or canvas. To make the seat more comfortable, position a thin layer of fabric wadding (batting) on top of the trunk lid before you cover it with fabric.

This colourful foam cube makes a cosy seat in a child's bedroom. Foam cubes are available in a range of sizes from foam supply shops. As a guide, we used a cube measuring 40 × 40 × 40 cm (16 × 16 × 16 in). Alphabet letters are perfect for the nursery but you can use flowers, boats or animal shapes, or spell out your child's name. Enlarge the template letters on pages 124–25 to the size required using a photocopier. We used fleece fabric because it is easy to stitch and does not fray, but if you want a more robust fabric, go for canvas or heavy-duty cotton.

alphabet seat

1 Measure the foam cube and cut two squares of fleece large enough to fit the top and bottom. Cut four more shapes for the sides, making them the same length but around 2 cm (⅞ in) wider to allow for a joining seam.

2 For the alphabet motif, draw the letters in reverse onto the fusible bonding web. Cut out the letters and iron them onto the contrasting piece of fleece fabric.

3 Iron the alphabet letters into place on the squares of fabric that will cover the cube. Stitch into place by hand, or use a sewing machine.

4 Working on the reverse of the fleece fabric, join together the four rectangles along both sides to make the sides of the cover. Pin and stitch the square for the top and trim the corners as necessary. Turn the cover right side out.

5 Pull the cover over the cube and turn it upside down. Attach the final square of fleece and handstitch in place, leaving two sides unstitched so that the cover can easily be removed for washing.

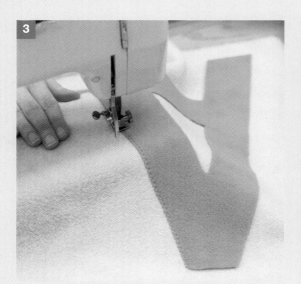

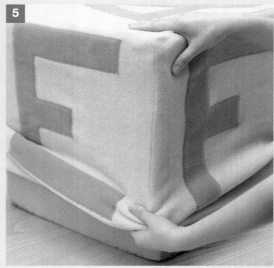

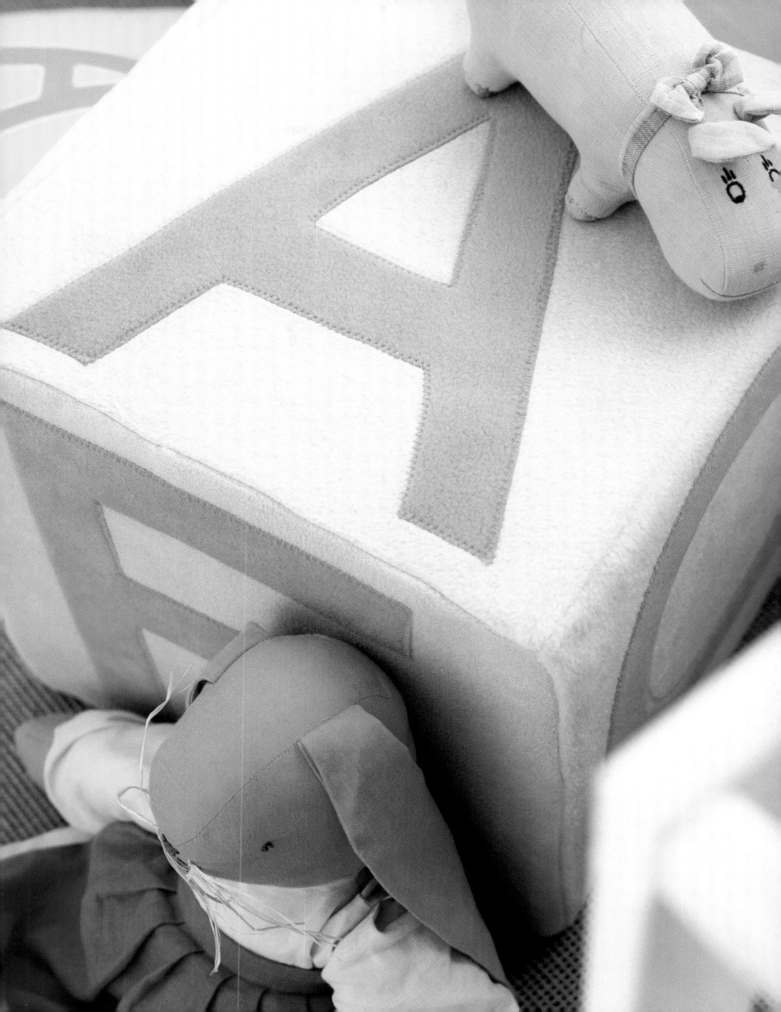

This sweet sheep motif is easy to add to a changing mat or fleece cot (crib) blanket and there is very little sewing involved. If you use a smaller template, you can create a small flock of sheep running around the edge of the material. The same motif could also be added to toy storage bags or ironed onto a square of canvas to create a cheerful wall hanging.

counting sheep

YOU WILL NEED

Fusible bonding web

Small piece of cream fleece fabric

Scissors

Black iron-on mending fabric

Sewing thread

Fleece cot (crib) blanket

1 Using the sheep templates below and enlarging them if necessary using a photocopier, draw the shape of the sheep's fleece onto the fusible bonding web. Cut out the shape, iron it onto the back of the cream fleece fabric, and cut out the fleece shape. For the sheep's body, use the template again, and mark the outline of the sheep onto the black iron-on mending fabric. Cut out as before.

2 Iron the body of the sheep onto the cot blanket. Finish by ironing the sheep's fleece onto the middle of the body and then stitch the sheep outline into place by hand or with a sewing machine.

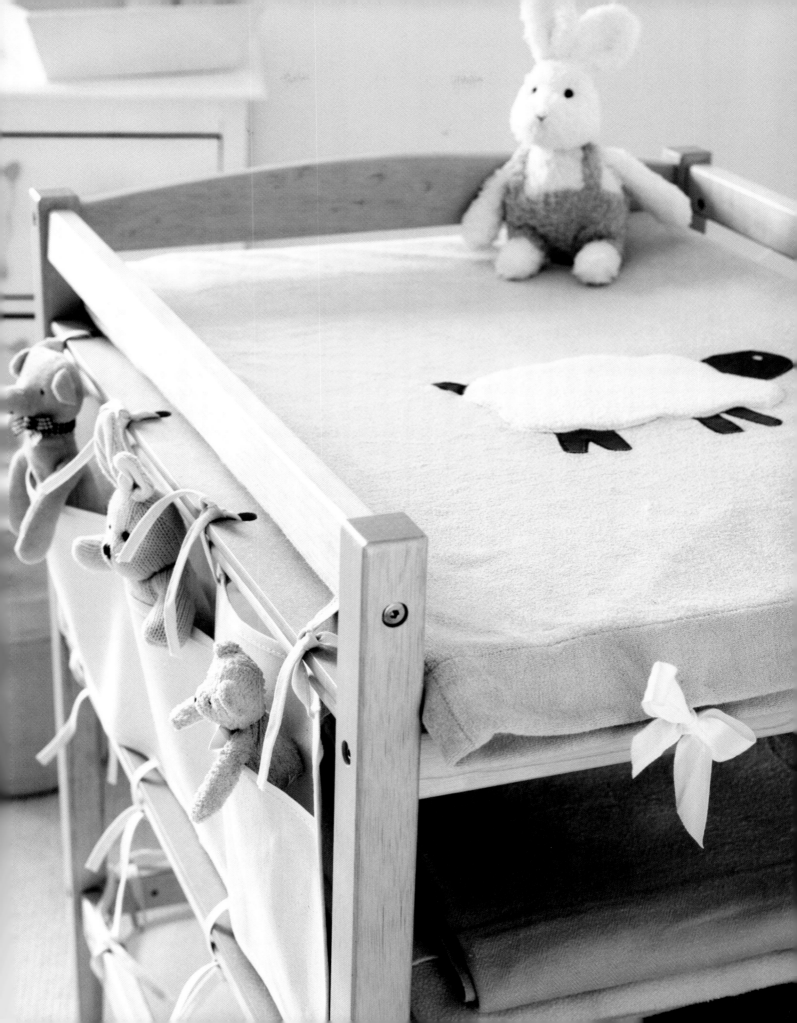

Jazz up plain bed linen with colourful spotty motifs. It is easy to create this fun bed linen by attaching colourful fabric shapes – and there is very little sewing involved. We chose simple spots in two colours – squares or rectangles would work just as well. You can dye plain white bed linen (use washing machine dye) so that it matches your room scheme perfectly.

spot the dots

YOU WILL NEED

Pencil

Circular object to draw around, such as a plate

Fusible bonding web

Scissors

Iron

Colourful cotton fabric remnants

Plain duvet cover and pillowcases

Embroidery thread

Embroidery needle

1 Using the pencil and circular shape, trace circles onto the fusible bonding web. Cut out the circles and iron them onto the cotton fabric remnants to bond them together then cut out the fabric circles. Map out the position of the circles on your duvet cover and pillowcases and peel off the paper backing. Iron the circles into position.

2 Create a blanket stitch border around the circles using embroidery thread and a needle. If you have any leftover circles, stick them to a square of fabric and frame them as a simple wall decoration.

DOTS AND DASHES Fabric painting pens are an even simpler way of transforming plain bed linen. Create a random spot design for the duvet cover and multi-coloured stripes for the pillowcase. Children will love to help out with this project and it's more effective if it looks hand-painted so don't worry too much about straight lines or uniform spots. Once you have created a design you like, fix it permanently in place with a hot iron. The painted designs look most effective against pale colour fabric such as white, cream or pale yellow.

TIP: You can buy sheeting fabric in a range of bright colours if you want to make a duvet cover from scratch. Simply measure an existing duvet cover and cut the sheeting to twice its width plus a little extra for seams. Fold over, seam on the top and remaining long side, and turn inside out. Add poppers, Velcro or fabric ties to the bottom edge for the opening.

Make your child's room into a retreat

A child's bedroom is a retreat from the big bad world, so it is important to create a space where your child can take ownership and feel secure enough to wind down after a day of super-charged activity.

Children love to feel grown-up so introduce adult-style pieces such as comfy scaled-down armchairs or a miniature sofa. Add bookshelves and magazine racks so your child feels comfortable in the room.

Enlist your child's help when re-organizing toys and other items – that way your child will know where to look without having to ask you all the time.

Encourage regular clean-outs and invite your child to help decide what must go. Telling your child that the toys or games are going to another child who needs them usually inspires thoughtful sacrifices and makes your child feel helpful.

Provide a secure place – a lockable jewellery box or drawer – for keeping the most valuable objects from the rest of the family. This is particularly important if your child has siblings who might be tempted to borrow a favourite toy, raid a piggybank or read a diary.

Locks on doors are not a good idea when children are young, but a 'Keep Out' or 'Please Knock' sign is a good way of establishing the principle that this is a personal space.

Let your child help with the decorating. You may not trust him or her with the walls, but even small children can paint artworks, help to decorate a cushion, or help choose an object of furniture. All these things foster pride in a child's surroundings and encourage them to look after their own belongings.

Chaos happens in children's rooms, but establish the principle that your child tidies up and makes the bed every day. Help your child with these jobs when he or she is still young enough to think housework is fun and you will reap the benefits later.

Painted chairs are useful as bedside tables or occasional seating so your child can entertain friends or host a tea party. Mix and match colours to make the effect bright and informal.

create your own art

Let your child stamp his or her identity by creating a personal work of art. They might decide on a self-portrait, or draw a favourite toy or pet. Canvases can be bought quite cheaply and children will love to see their masterpiece hung on the wall.

YOU WILL NEED

Fabric painting pens

Canvas

1 Lay the canvas on newspaper or an old sheet and let your child map out a design using fabric painting pens, which look similar to felt-tip pens and are easy to use.

2 Once the ink is dry, run a hot iron over the top to create a permanent design.

DECORATOR'S NOTE

Get all the marker pens back after the art session or your furniture could get an unwelcome makeover.

CHAPTER 4

themed rooms

From fairies to farmyard animals,
create a fantasy land by designing
their room around a well-loved theme

Marvellous menageries

Create your room scheme

The best starting point is to find a fabric or wallpaper to inspire you and then base your colour scheme around that. Don't feel it has to be all animals or soft colours – this is a look that blends happily with bold stripes, spots, flowers and alphabet letters.

Mix animal motifs

Cut-out animal motifs are an easy way to transform plain furniture. Paint with vinyl matt emulsion (latex) or acrylic paint and stick the motifs onto furniture with glue, or use Velcro squares for easy removal when your child has moved on to another theme. You can create your own simple motifs from thin plywood or MDF (composite board) using a jigsaw. Don't restrict the shapes to furniture – they look good on walls and doors too, and make excellent templates if you want to continue the same design by adding stencilled or fabric shapes to plain cushions and pillowcases.

From farmyard chickens to cuddly dogs or exotic zoo creatures, animal-themed rooms are a perennial favourite with both boys and girls. They are adaptable too, working just as well in the nursery as they do for older children. The real beauty of this theme is that you are not tied to a particular colour or style – and you will find the elements that make the look work are easy to source.

If you want to use paint decoratively, why not create a border effect? Start with a base of yellow, then mask off part of the wall and create zigzag stripes in darker green paint to suggest a farmer's meadow. Add flower or animal stickers or MDF (composite board) motifs to complete the look.

Soft blues and aquas work well with dreamy farmyard scenes in nurseries. Remember that very young babies respond more to shape and texture than they do to strong colours, so go for tactile materials and textured effects on soft furnishings. Mix in plenty of white or cream – or soft yellow – to add warmth and to keep the setting relaxing.

Bolder shades of yellow and red blend well in older children's rooms – particularly if the room is filled with exotic wild creatures. Add stripes or spots to mimic the patterns on animal coats and introduce lush greens to conjure a jungle habitat.

As an easy alternative to borders and wallpaper, look for large animal design stickers and group them together in a square or line to create an instant feature wall. This works particularly well if you opt for simple graphic designs.

MOVEABLE BLACKBOARD

Let your child draw a chalk menagerie on the floor with this clever blackboard on wheels. You will need to get a circle of MDF (composite board) cut to size by a wood merchant (lumberyard). Sand it lightly (wear a protective mask and do this in a well-ventilated area), prime with MDF primer, and paint it with specialist blackboard paint. Screw on four sturdy castors for easy movement. If you prefer a fixed drawing board, the blackboard paint can also be used on bare or painted wood, making it ideal for the back of the door or for painting on a tabletop.

make a simple mobile

Animal mobiles are easy to create for yourself using a padded coat hanger.

YOU WILL NEED

Padded coat hanger

Ribbon

Soft toys/felt

1 Use colourful ribbon to hang small soft toys from the hanger, or stitch your own animal shapes using brightly coloured felt. If you prefer a round mobile, use a circular wooden ring instead. Wind fabric or ribbon around the ring before attaching your animals with ribbon or cord.

2 Use the sturdy hook to attach the mobile to the ceiling. Position the mobile out of reach of very young children, particularly if it is hung above a cot.

MIX AND MATCH DESIGNS

If you are choosing a strong base colour such as deep blue, the bedroom can feel dark, so include plenty of white or cream on furniture and accessories to lighten the effect. Mix and match patterns with similar background colours as this also helps to stop the base colour from becoming overpowering. Consider adding an additional accent shade such as deep pink or silver on a few well-chosen details to create points of interest and to stop the room becoming over-coordinated. Although the curtains and bed linen here carry a cute dog motif, the wallpaper is a simple spot design, making it easy to update the scheme in future by introducing new soft furnishings.

Add animal details

From flocks of sheep to cowhide prints, introduce a menagerie of animal accessories to make this theme really come to life.

- Add menagerie-themed posters, or ask your child to draw some favourite animals and then frame the artworks. Try your local history museum for postcards and posters with a zoological theme. If you prefer a softer look, frame a square of colourful animal motif wallpaper or fabric.

- Introduce animals to plain furniture and accessories – a stencilled design on a chest of drawers or chair, or a stamped motif on a plain lampshade will tie your scheme together nicely.

- Mobiles look particularly effective if you choose designs in strong colours or light-reflecting materials and hang them near a window to catch the breeze.

- Look for neat extras such as pin boards or wall hooks to complete the look. You could paint or stencil a simple animal shape on the wall and attach sturdy coat hooks by the animal's feet or nose.

Sail away

Nautical rooms tap into children's love of the sea and provide the perfect opportunity to take the beachcomber approach to decorating; add flotsam and jetsam collected on your travels, such as model boats, seashells and brightly painted buckets and spades. This look appeals equally to boys and girls. You can take the classic blue-and-white approach or go for a sunny beach holiday flavour with flashes of sand yellow or pink, and brilliant deck chair stripes.

Create your room scheme

The base colour is almost always blue (and nearly any shade will do), which you can lighten with crisp white or brighten with nautical prints, deck chair stripes or bold flashes of red.

- Choose a soft white or cream with a flat matt finish for walls, and introduce layers of colour in curtains and bed linen. For an underwater feel, decorate the room in a rich marine blue and lighten the effect by choosing paler colours through details.

- Sailing boat-, fish- or seabird-patterned wallpapers all work well, but look for small motifs or paint walls and add a border so you can be bold with accessories.

- Bunk or cabin beds add an instant below-decks flavour – especially if you add a nautical-patterned duvet cover or hang a flag from the ceiling. Look for bed designs in plain or painted wood to create the illusion that this is a ship's cabin.

- Mid-coloured wood furniture or distressed driftwood-style white finishes set the scene perfectly. Look for unusual nautical-themed pieces such as a bookshelf shaped like an upturned boat. Striped canvas also works well – especially for beach hut-style wardrobes and bedside cupboards.

- Floors can be practical wood or cork, or use natural flooring such as sisal in a soft sand shade. To add more comfort underfoot, look for fish or boat-shaped rugs or go for a plain rug in red or blue.

- Curtains and blinds can be in plain or deck chair-striped canvas or look for timeless designs with boats and fish. Add rope cord tiebacks decorated with fish or starfish to curtains. You could even try adding a few sailors' knots along the length of the tiebacks.

nautical-themed shelves

Plain painted shelves get a marine flavour if you add a wave-effect MDF (composite board) trim. You can buy ready-made trim or make it yourself using a jigsaw.

YOU WILL NEED

Ready-made trim

Glue/screws

Paint

Hooks

1 Glue or screw the trim onto a shelf and paint it to match the wood, or decorate in a bold contrast such as white. Here, the shelves are used to display a range of treasures – buckets in ice cream shades plus shells and other found objects in blue box frames.

2 Add hooks below the shelves for stowing canvas beach bags or clothes.

Add seafaring details

Capture life on the coast with marine-inspired accessories. Choose objects that are fun and bright to conjure up seaside holidays and exciting ocean journeys to far-flung shores.

- You can really have fun with details, adding a life buoy wall decoration, flags or seabirds and fish in plain or painted wood.

- Introduce a sense of light and space by adding round, porthole-style mirrors – metallic or white-painted frames look most effective.

- Introduce child-sized deck chairs or colourful floor cushions for seating. Hang a hammock if you think it will be safe enough for your child.

- Add images of starfish, whales or old nautical maps to the walls. Stencil simple images of seabirds in flight onto squares of cream canvas, mount in driftwood-style frames and group together.

- An old wooden or wicker trunk makes the perfect treasure chest for toys and games, while bright canvas or towelling bags can be slung from the bedstead or hung behind the door. Make your own designs using rectangular offcuts of colourful canvas or cotton and add plain white or blue rope cord handles.

- Lighting can be simple, with white canvas shades and pale or plain wood stands. Or look for a lighthouse-style stand for the bedside table and decorate the shade with seagull motifs using a fabric-painting pen.

- Encourage your child to help collect and decorate accessories for the bedroom. Introduce a line of painted pebbles or a collection of driftwood along the windowsill, or fill a plain jar with sand, and place it on the bookshelf: this can be a reminder of your last beach holiday.

PAINT FEATURE DOORS

Add stripes to turn plain wooden doors into a focal point. Use a plumb line to create the stripes. Start by painting the doors in the palest shade (in this case, yellow), then mask off the areas to be painted in a darker contrast shade using a plumb line and ruler to ensure you get a straight, vertical line. Once you have created a two-tone effect, finish by adding a thin blue stripe to create a beach hut effect. The metal portholes were added before the doors were painted.

Stars and spaceships

Using the night sky as your inspiration, create a colourful star-spangled setting where your child can plot his or her next journey into space. This is a look based around blue, but introduce flashes of silver or bold yellow to set the cosmic mood, or paint the walls neutral and add an intergalactic border, bold bed linen and futuristic accessories.

Night-sky backdrop

Deep tones of blue set the scene for a room that comes to life once the lights go out. Add glow-in-the-dark sticker stars to the ceiling and walls to create a twinkling night-sky effect. Details such as cheerful star-shaped cushions make the room come to life in the daytime and you can suspend model rockets from the ceiling or add a border decorated with spaceships, comets or astronauts.

Add a galaxy to furniture

Transform a plain table by adding a galaxy of stars. Paint a table in your chosen base colour (dark blue or grey is best). Use a star stencil and yellow paint to create your design. If you prefer a glittering finish, choose a metallic silver or gold paint. Paint the stars all over the table or use sparingly to create a random or border effect. Add a rocket or two if you want to make this a space scene. Apply two coats of clear matt varnish to protect the design once it is completed.

Introduce space-age lighting

A rocket-shaped bedside lamp is a fun finishing touch. Alternatively, add a lampshade shaped like a half-moon to the ceiling. A string of twinkling fairy lights strung along the ceiling will add to the cosmic aura of the room.

◀◀ *Moon rocket bedlinen sets the scene.*

◀ *This tabletop gets a cosmic makeover.*

▶ *Yellow star cushions and stencils add flashes of bright colour.*

▶ *Look for space-age accessories such as a lava lamp.*

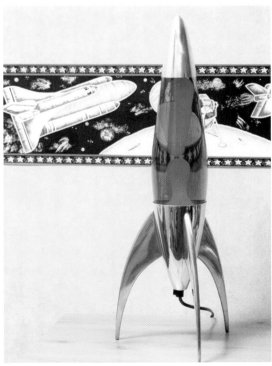

Sporting legends

You cannot choose the team your child supports – or the strip that goes with it – so sports-themed rooms are usually a riot of traffic-stopping shades. But you can still add clever details to make this a winning setting that everybody loves. The trick is to combine favourite colours and beloved sporting memorabilia with more understated elements including areas of plain neutral wall, timeless wooden furniture and small-scale patterns such as checks and stripes.

Stick to the strip

Use your favourite team's colours on bed linen and walls – you will probably find a whole host of themed merchandise to make this easier. If the colours threaten to become overpowering, temper the effect by creating one feature wall in a bold shade and paint the other walls in white or cream. Here, a predominantly red strip is combined with a blue-and-red striped rug, while a red-and-white checked cushion decorates the bedside chair. A simple soccer motif border frames the wall behind the bed head and a lucky pair of soccer boots is hung from the wall.

Introduce simple neutral details

Plain oak furniture in simple, pared-down designs stops the team strip from dominating the whole room. Add neutral carpet to make the room feel lighter and to ensure that it outlasts the current craze. You can also introduce a sense of light by fitting a dado rail halfway up the wall and painting the area above it in a cool, neutral colour and the section below in a team colour. Simple accessories such as a colourful banner or scarf help to keep heroes in the frame.

Customize accessories

It's easy to introduce team colours via furniture and accessories – and these can easily be repainted a few years down the line. A plain wall cupboard can be decorated in the team strip, or you could add stickers or photos to a tabletop or mirror frame. Introduce a special display area – a large pin board with a frame painted in the home team colours is ideal for hanging tickets, flags and other mementoes.

◄◄ *Checked and striped soft furnishings blend happily with team colours.*

◄ *A bold red soccer strip is paired with areas of neutral wall and plain wood furniture.*

Think pink

Nearly every little girl loves pink – after all, it is the colour of choice for princesses, ballet dancers, Barbie and other favourite characters – so this theme is your chance to create a delicious girlie setting your child will love. Restraint doesn't really come into it when you are sourcing fluffy pink cushions and gossamer-light voile, so get into the spirit of fairy-tale endings and enjoy the chance to relive the imaginative world of your own childhood.

Create your room scheme

Think pink by mixing and matching hues from the rosy end of the spectrum. Combine the palest blush shades, ice cream, and bubble-gum pinks, with cerise and even rich red. If you want to make this a subtler setting, add lilac, lavender, cream or cowslip yellow.

Look for wallpapers featuring fairies, princesses and angels, but also cuddly animals and fairy-tale castles. For a softer effect, choose border paper instead or create one feature wall behind the bed. Pink can be cold over large areas if you get the wrong shade, so choose colours with reddish tones (rather than blue or lilac tones) to keep the effect light and warm.

Luxury is a key feature for this theme, so choose soft textures underfoot with carpet in a neutral colour. White-painted or wooden floorboards also work well, provided you add deep-pile rugs.

Soft cream- or white-painted furniture works best (avoid shiny surfaces or dark wood), so choose French-style pieces with curved legs and scrolled edges. Or look for rustic, stripped-pine furniture to create a timeless, country-style setting.

ADD SIMPLE HEART STENCILS

Simple stencilled or stamped hearts are easy to create and you can use them to highlight a focal point on the wall such as a display shelf, or to frame a bed. Group together and choose a deep pink or reddish hue. If you want to add a really romantic feel, use metallic stencil paint in gold or silver to outline, or add stick-on sequins in metallic pink. You can continue the romantic theme on soft furnishings using stamps and fabric paint or by drawing outline hearts on plain white pillowcases or cushion covers with fabric painting pens.

HANG UNUSUAL DECORATIONS

Pictures of angels, fairies or turreted castles create a romantic theme. For something different, hang 3D objects – a pair of jewelled ballet shoes or fairy wings pinned to the wall add instant glamour. Secure firmly from a picture hook using thin cord or picture wire. It is best to hang objects well out of reach if your child is at an age when she is likely to give tempting objects a good tug.

95

CREATE A VOILE CANOPY

It is easy to buy ready-made canopies or make your own using a length of lightweight fabric. To make a canopy, attach a fabric tie to the material then screw a hook to the ceiling to drape it. An alternative is to attach the panel to the wall with a hook or a ready-made half coronet. Drape the fabric on either side of the bed head or along the whole length of the bed for a really dreamy effect. You may find it easier to get the billowing-folds effect if you stitch a thin wood or wire ring underneath the material close to the top of the canopy. Voile is the best material for canopies because it's both lightweight and translucent. Choose white, pale pink or lavender and look out for designs with subtle flower or fairy prints.

Sugar and candy themes make a good alternative to traditional fairies. Look for images featuring ice cream cupcakes or other 1950s-style graphic motifs. Add candy stripe patterns and soft buttercream woodwork to create a setting that looks good enough to eat.

Add romantic details

A silky bed throw is the ultimate in fairy-tale luxury. Look for an offcut of luxurious material (heavy curtain fabric is ideal). Alternatively, make a reversible throw by stitching together two pieces of fabric in harmonious colours such as pink and red. Add bead- or sequin-trimmed edges.

Padded seating such as soft beanbags, miniature armchairs or sofas makes the room feel comfortable. Add a pretty dressing table (see pages 98–99) or wardrobe to make the space feel grown-up.

Introduce different textures to add interest to soft furnishings. Look for cushions with silky, knitted or plush finishes and mix them with crisp cotton gingham or a pattern that complements the curtains.

Choose soft, ambient lighting, a string of fairy lights hung around the bed or a bedside light with a ruched fabric shade.

Window treatments should be romantic, so choose elegant voile drapes or pretty patterned fabric. Add a plain or patterned blind behind to shut out the light. Add details such as gingham bow tiebacks.

97

TRY HOT PINK FOR GROWN-UP STYLE

If you want to create a variation on the fairy-tale theme that will appeal to older girls, then turn up the heat. This is a look that relies on a restricted palette of two colours, but it can work all the way up to your child's teen years provided you dare to be bold! We chose a pale pink for the walls and strong cerise pink accents for bed linen, rug and accessories. There is no pattern in this scheme to dilute the effect, although hints of romance are added with the fairy-tale canopy and pretty ballerina dress as wall decoration. With such a simple two-tone scheme, it is easy to make changes simply by altering the accent colour of your accessories.

A plain table gets the country-garden look with wallpaper motifs.
The motifs can be cottage-garden flowers or you could opt for a
more contemporary design using circles or squares.

petal power table

YOU WILL NEED

Dressing table

Vinyl matt emulsion
(latex)

Paintbrush

Wallpaper or wallpaper
offcuts

Scissors

PVA glue

Artist's brush

Damp sponge

Acrylic varnish

1 Prepare the table (sanding if necessary)
and apply two coats of vinyl matt emulsion.

2 Carefully cut out the motifs and set aside.
Group the motifs as you cut out; this will
make it easier to plan your design as you work.

3 Thin a little PVA glue with water until it
has the consistency of cream. Apply the glue
onto the back of a motif. Place the motif on
the table, press down with a damp sponge to
secure it in place and wipe off any excess glue.
Do this lightly and firmly, but don't rub or you
will risk tearing the wallpaper. Repeat to cover
the tabletop, legs and drawers.

4 Once the motifs are dry, apply at least three
coats of acrylic varnish to secure in place.

TRY STENCILS OR STAMPS: If cutting out
and sticking looks too much like hard work,
use a stencil or stamp to achieve a similar
effect. This works particularly well if you
pick out a colour and motif to match the
curtains or bed linen.

DECORATOR'S NOTE: Try placing the motifs
and mark the positions with a pencil before
you start gluing. We chose a random, scattered
flowers pattern, but you could restrict your
design to the centre of the tabletop or just
apply it to the drawer fronts.

Children at work

Trucks and cranes are all sources of wonder to small children, and what looks like a dusty building site to you is fascinating to them. Here are some simple ways to introduce a transport theme to your child's room.

Combine lively patterns

A line of trucks circling the wall or a digger-decorated duvet cover will provide hours of fun as your child imagines him- or herself in the driver's seat, and this look is perfect for younger transport enthusiasts. Choose cheerful contrasts such as red and blue, and paint furniture to match the bed linen and curtains. Toys can provide decorative finishing touches, so make plenty of space to display favourite cars and trucks.

Choose industrial colours

Bright 'hazard' colours such as yellow and red are perfect for setting this scene. You can add details such as miniature yellow hard hats, warning stickers (available from builder's merchants or home improvement retailers), and industrial-style open shelving to display favourite trucks and diggers. Here, a feature wall was created using red and white chevrons, and woodwork was transformed with a yellow-and-white banded pattern to replicate the barrier tape used on building sites.

▲ *This red and blue patterned room has a bedside cupboard painted in coordinating colours.*

◀ *Combine bright hazard colours to create a construction site bedroom.*

Paint a truck mural

This mural is the ultimate treat for a transport-mad child and it is easy to create a professional finish if you use a few tricks. Make sure you choose a bold and simple design with plenty of straight edges so you can mark out your design on the wall first. If you are a confident artist, do this freehand with a ruler, using an image from a book or magazine as your guide. For less confident artists, it is much easier if you use a slide projector. Project your chosen image onto the wall, enlarge it until it is the size you want, and use to create your outlines in pencil. With the outlines in place, fill in the detail, using your image as a reference while you paint. Work from the bottom upwards, painting the larger areas first before adding the details. Use acrylic-based paint and go over areas of the mural if you are not happy with your handiwork. Add a clear varnish finish once the mural is finished and dry.

▼ *Bold graphic designs make effective murals – use strong colours for maximum impact.*

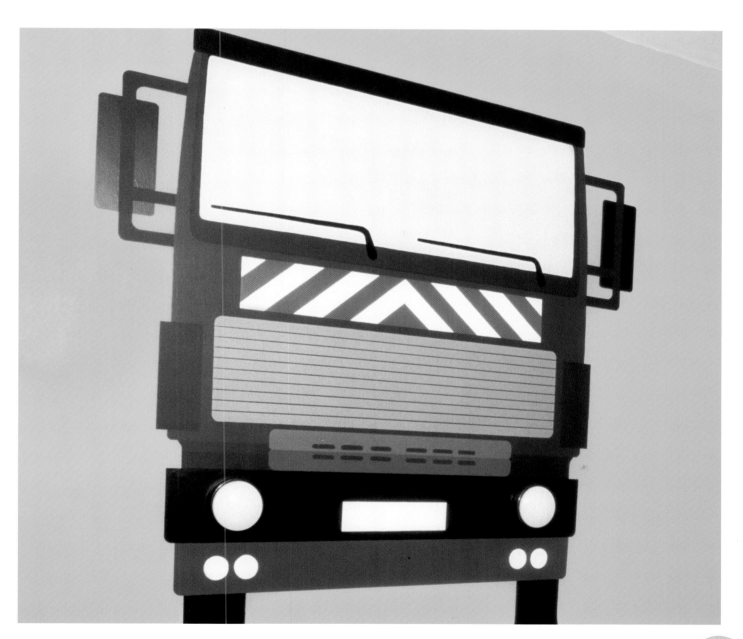

Comic book heroes

Even older children enjoy sharing a room with a favourite movie or comic strip hero. Decorating around such a familiar theme is easiest if you buy ready-made bed linen, but you can still add clever details to make the room feel more personal.

Add clever details

There is something sinister about Spiderman's arm appearing over the back of the door – a perfect joke feature to please children. If you are confident about painting, mark out the image in pencil on the door using a photo or picture as a guide. Alternatively, photocopy your design and enlarge it to create the template on the back of the door.

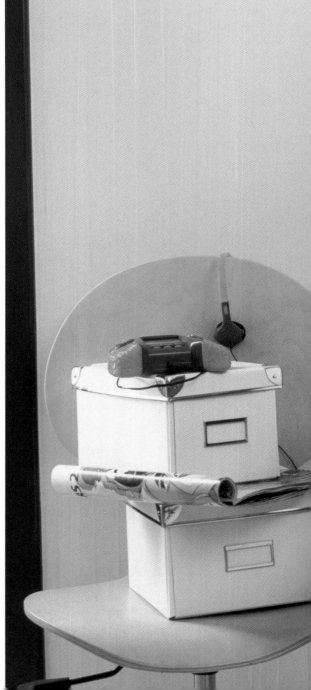

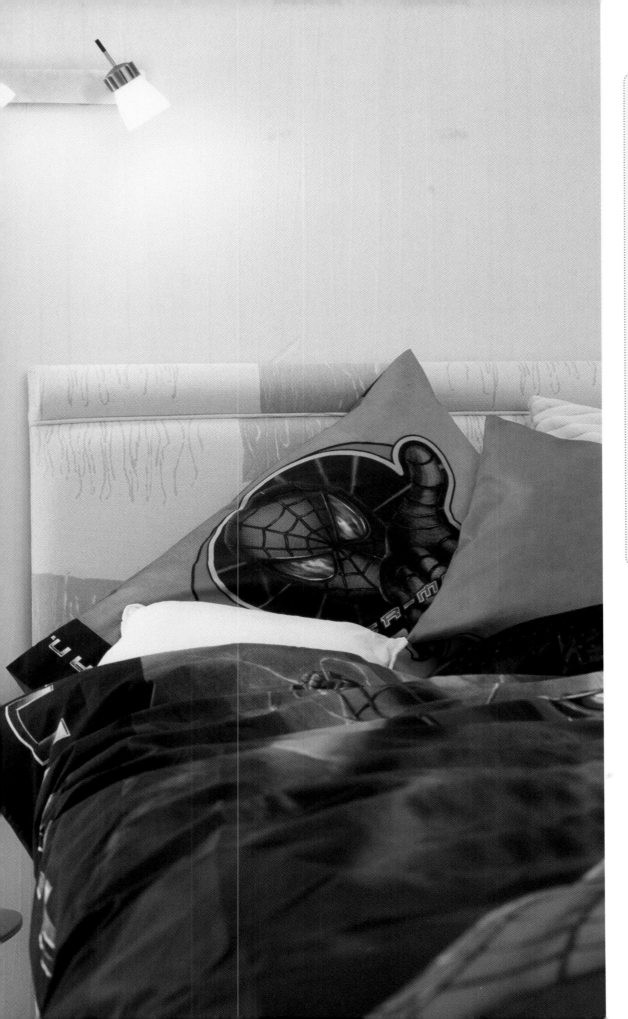

CHOOSE BOLD BED LINEN

Keep the colour scheme simple if you choose a bed linen as colourful as this red and black Spiderman design. The walls are painted in a neutral shade and contemporary lighting and furniture complement the bold graphic design of the soft furnishings. Add in red-framed pictures or combine red with black in accessories such as cushions and storage boxes to reinforce the theme. A red and black rug on the floor or a red-trimmed blind is the only finishing touch you need to complete the look.

This is a simple version of decoupage using large pieces of comic. Choose a favourite comic book hero and you are guaranteed to create a table your child will enjoy using. An older child will enjoy helping with this project, and may even decide to do it him- or herself.

loony cartoons table

YOU WILL NEED

Coffee table

Three or four comics (depending on size of table)

PVA glue

Paintbrush

1 Tear the comics into pieces, leaving some pages whole, and ripping others into two or four pieces. You can be as neat or as jumbled as you like.

2 Using a paintbrush, coat a small area of the table with PVA glue, then stick down a few pieces of comic. Repeat the process in small sections until you have covered the table with the comic.

3 When all the pieces are stuck down, create a hardwearing finish by painting over the table with PVA glue diluted with water (about one part water to three parts glue). Leave to dry overnight.

TRY STICKERS: If you prefer a simpler decoration technique, add stickers to the table. For younger children this is an ideal way to bedeck a piece of furniture with their favourite cartoon characters. Make sure the surface is clean and dry (it may help to key it with fine-grade sandpaper and then wipe with a damp cloth). Once the stickers have been applied, finish with a protective coat of PVA glue diluted with water, as before.

DECORATOR'S NOTE: Although we chose old issues of a colourful children's comic, this would work just as well with a sci-fi, sports or pony magazine – you could even use copies of family photographs. Make sure the table is clean and smooth before you start gluing. If you prefer, leave the legs plain and cover just the tabletop with images. Use the same technique to decorate plain box files or a wooden mirror frame.

CHAPTER 5

make a bedroom into a den

Add grown-up details to suit their

changing tastes and create a

space where they feel at home

Changing tastes

Children grow up fast and all too soon the cute farmyard wallpaper or fairy duvet cover is pronounced babyish. Before you have had time to adjust to this grown-up attitude, the 'Keep Out' sign has been hung on the door and your child's bedroom has become a no-go zone. This can be an awkward phase as children make the transition from child to teenager. One day your child is being super-cool and the next, they spend a happy afternoon rediscovering long-lost toys – your challenge is to accommodate familiar childhood possessions and make space for teenage hobbies and preoccupations. It is important to re-examine the space to ensure your child has room to study and to entertain friends.

Choosing a new look

There is no point losing sleep trying to work out what your 'tweenie' wants the bedroom to become. You cannot possibly because you are an adult, and are therefore, by definition, uncool. You are also immune to peer-pressure, teen magazines and other factors that influence your child's decision-making. Take your child to a home store or provide brochures, paint cards and magazines, and ask if he or she can show you images that appeal. Be prepared to ask them to compromise – particularly since a passion for black or metallic purple could evaporate almost as soon as the paint is dry.

▲ *Soft pink is paired with a lilac stripe on bed linen, border and rug for a sophisticated look.*

◀ *White walls, smart accessories and a simple striped duvet cover give this room a sophisticated edge.*

▶ *Office-style accessories create a practical study and sleep zone.*

Adapt an existing scheme

Assess whether a total redecoration is essential. It could be possible to simply adapt the room to appear more grown-up. Minor changes are cheaper and many can be undertaken in a few hours. Here are quick revamps to consider.

Dilute the colour scheme

If the room is painted in a colour your child no longer likes, consider minimizing its effect. Do this by introducing additional colours or changing details such as the duvet cover and blind. It is generally safest to stick with toning or harmonious shades.

Add neutral white or cream

If the colours in the room are bold, your options are restricted, but white and cream are fail-safe choices that update a scheme and make it seem more sophisticated. Paint one or two walls neutral to soften the impact, or introduce white or cream above a picture or dado rail. Add neutral furniture and bed linen to create a similar effect.

Try metallics

Silver and metallic finishes are effective ways of making a room appear contemporary; they reflect the light and give a lift to colour schemes that feel dark or dull. Add mirrors, chrome storage stands or introduce a metallic border or sticker shapes to the walls.

Streamline the room

Clearing out the clutter is one of the fastest ways to update a dated room. Encourage your child to get rid of unwanted toys and games with the promise that you will go shopping for new furniture and accessories. Office supply shops are a great source of functional pieces such as desks and open shelves. Combine these with office-style accessories and add in a few luxury details such as a comfy chair, smart table lamps and a co-ordinating rug to create a streamlined study and sleeping zone.

REPLACE A DATED BORDER

Character wallpapers are one of the first things your child is likely to outgrow. You cannot avoid redecorating if all four walls are wallpapered, but a border can be simple to remove if the plaster underneath is sound. Use a wallpaper stripper and soak the paper thoroughly before peeling it away gently. You may be able to add a new border, or paint on a border effect to cover any marks and imperfections the paper leaves behind. Here, a simple border in orange decorated by reflective circle motifs adds a smart twist to the bedroom of a pre-teen.

Mix patterns with plains

Bridge the gap between child and teenager by painting the walls in a bold shade. Go for a colour your child will love and that can be mixed easily with a variety of shades. Introduce interest through patterned bed linen and clever accessories. You can update this scheme easily by changing bed linen and details.

Create a blank canvas

If it is impossible to get a decision out of your child or you are not comfortable with his or her colour choice, consider painting the walls plain white and accessorize with the chosen shade. You could add a third accent colour with smaller details. Mix bold, plain elements with patterns that include white (for instance checks or stripes) so the scheme feels unified.

◄ *With its plain blue walls and simple iron bedstead, this girl's room can be adapted quite easily by introducing different bed linen.*

Flexible designs

If you have decided it is time to redecorate, you need to choose a design that will outlast the next few crazes. This has to be a look that feels more grown-up, without it being pronounced boring. Most older children still love colour and pattern – they are just wary of anything that could be viewed by their friends as childish. Here are some pointers.

▶ *White can be partnered with almost any colour you like, provided you pick up the white in patterns elsewhere in the room. Here, white is used to dramatic effect by combining it with a bold, red, bedside cabinet, and subtle checks and spots on the rug and bed linen.*

Turn up the heat

Bold yellow or hot orange may leave you reaching for sunglasses but they are practical choices for children who love bright colours. They are easy to accessorize with cooler blues and greens. This combination creates a stimulating environment without a childish feel. These tropical shades work equally well for boys' and girls' rooms, making them a safe option for shared playrooms.

Choose elegant wallpaper

There is no need to restrict your choice to the children's section of the wallpaper books. Provided you choose a pattern that contains your child's favourite shades, you can choose a muted floral or spotted backdrop that won't look out of place in the room when he or she is older. Change the accessories to update the room at a later time.

A ROOM FOR A GIRL

If you don't want to abandon the girly look in your daughter's room just yet, purple makes a good choice. It has all the feminine qualities of pink but can be made sophisticated with pale lilac. You can add a canopy around the bed for now (choose a violet-coloured voile) and remove it when your daughter is older. Here, a graphic circle border is placed at picture rail height and the same shape is picked out in the silver-framed porthole mirror below it. Open storage by the bed is a practical space to store jewellery and accessories and makes a simple alternative to a dressing table. Purple works well with silver, so you can add metallic and chrome elements to reflect light, and increase study and storage space.

stick-on flower lantern

Use fake flowers to dress up a simple paper lantern. We chose exotic orchids but you could go for simpler blooms, such as daisies or cornflowers that pick out existing colours or motifs in your room scheme.

YOU WILL NEED

Paper lampshade

Fake flowers (we used silk orchids)

Scissors/craft knife

Glue gun

1 Open up the lampshade and hang it securely from a broom handle or pole so you can attach the flowers.

2 Cut the stalks off the fake flowers using scissors or a craft knife.

3 Attach the flowers to the lampshade using a glue gun. Use a random pattern for the best effect and do not apply too much glue – it looks very effective if the petals can flutter in the breeze.

bold foil-motif walls

These stick-on silver shapes are a great way to liven up plain painted walls and to introduce a bold flash of silver to a plain room. You can use them to create a straight border, group them together like a piece of wall art or frame a bed or window.

YOU WILL NEED

Ruler

Pencil

Stick-on motifs

Dry cloth

1 Ensure the wall is clean and free from dust or grease. If it is recently painted, make sure it is thoroughly dry.

2 Decide where you want to position the motifs and use a ruler and pencil to create a horizontal guideline. Make sure you also create vertical guides to ensure the motifs will be positioned an equal distance apart. If you are not happy doing this by eye, use a plumb line and spirit level.

3 Carefully peel off the adhesive backing and position each motif lightly. Stand back and check the position again before you use a dry cloth to fix the motifs to the wall. Smooth out any pockets of air with the cloth.

▲ *Pick patterns and details that match your son's hobbies.*

◀ *Bold pattern mixing keeps the look informal.*

A ROOM FOR A BOY

Pared-back neutrals such as taupe and khaki green make an easy-going backdrop for a boy's room. They are safe and familiar colours for children who live in combat trousers and sports clothes and can be combined easily with stronger colours or toned down with white or cream.

Add interest to a neutral setting with subtle, patterned wallpaper. Add bolder designs on the windows and soft furnishings such as floor cushions. This is a look that is tailor-made for adapting as your child grows – for instance, by switching the curtains for plain, wooden Venetian blinds. The absence of fussy details is integral to its appeal, so avoid over-accessorizing or you'll lose the impression that this is a modern, streamlined space. An ultra-simple shelving unit along one wall provides room to store clothes and play on the computer, while simple patterned storage boxes make a neat stowaway for toys and games.

▼ *Allow plenty of open storage for sports gear and choose simple, functional furniture.*

This is a transformation you can make in an afternoon and it is a great way to give a contemporary feel to a plain wardrobe. The effect works best if you use a wardrobe that's already painted. Add silver wardrobe handles if you want to complete the glittering effect.

sparkly wardrobe

YOU WILL NEED

Tracing paper

Thick card

Scissors

Aluminium foil

Ballpoint pen

Scalpel or craft knife

Spray adhesive

1 Trace around the design and transfer the shape onto thick card. Cut this out to make a template. We chose a naive flower motif but stars, large circles or geometric shapes would work equally well.

2 Lay the foil on a flat surface and draw around the template with the pen, repeating the pattern until you get the required number of motifs.

3 Cut out the shapes and attach them to the top panels of the wardrobe using spray adhesive. We also nailed in a small silver tack to make the flower centre, but this is optional.

4 For the bottom panels, cut out foil pieces to fit the doors – you need to do this accurately so use a scalpel or craft knife to get straight edges without tearing the foil. Decorating is easy: trace around the template with a pen to get the indent effect. Finally, attach the foil pieces to the wardrobe doors using spray adhesive as before.

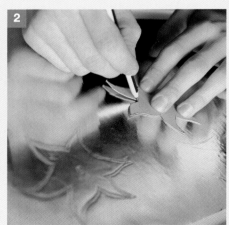

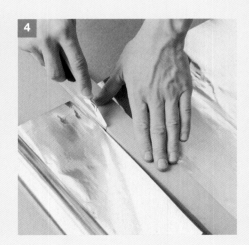

If you do not have space for a conventional desk, consider a design that fits in a cupboard. Choose one with racks or shelves inside the door to hold homework and other essentials – office supply companies are a good source of well-designed stowaway desks. Add a comfortable work chair – a lightweight metal design with a padded seat and back is the basic option. Ergonomic versions such as ball seats, posture and saddle stools are also worth considering, particularly as they do not take up much space. Or you can buy a height-adjustable office chair that can be adapted as your child grows. Whatever you choose, make sure it provides adequate back support.

Remember details such as a wrist support and footrest. Add task lighting close to the screen to avoid eyestrain.

Study, storage and seating

A desk space is very important once homework and school projects start to occupy your child's evenings and weekends. Here are watchpoints for a hard working room:

The basic essential is a desk big enough to hold a computer. This needs to be at a comfortable working height with the screen at eye-level to encourage good posture and prevent back or neck problems. Avoid angling the computer – your child should face it, rather than twisting to work. Choose a desk design with enough knee room plus space to keep papers and books open next to the computer. Look for space-making features such as pullout keyboard shelves.

Make home study fun

Help your child get organized with schoolwork by providing storage that is a pleasure to use. Utilize wall space above the computer and add drawer or filing areas below the desk.

- Introduce small storage items for holding disks, papers and project work neatly. This storage need not be utilitarian; look for bright colours and neat ideas such as cases with in-built storage dividers for holding arts and craft materials.

- Include colourful notice boards for pinning memos and invitations. You can make these easily by painting cork floor tiles with leftover emulsion (latex). Alternatively, cover with bright felt or cotton canvas.

- Position metal or wooden open shelves close to the desk and provide a range of colour-coordinated items such as magazine files and lidded boxes. This see-at-a-glance storage will encourage your child to get organized and to stay that way.

Provide plenty of seating

Make the room sociable by adding extra seating for friends. Your choice depends on space, but even the smallest room should be able to accommodate a floor cushion.

- Whatever chair you choose, it must be lightweight and contemporary. Armchairs, portable beanbags or fun plastic blow-up chairs are all good choices.

- If you have a large room, include a small side table for stowing magazines and books. This can form a useful divider between relaxation and sleep/work zones, particularly if you choose a practical unit with storage space underneath. A neat sofa bed or day bed makes a useful addition, since it can be converted when friends stay or at busy times like Christmas. If space is tight, look for a chair bed that provides a single, futon-style mattress.

PAINT, DYE & SPECIAL FINISHES

Products for walls and woodwork, plus specialist floor, fabric and multisurface lines.

Crown Paints: www.crownpaints.co.uk
Dulux: www.dulux.co.uk
Dylon: www.dylon.co.uk
Farrow & Ball: www.farrow-ball.co.uk
Fired Earth: www.firedearth.com
Fun2Do: www.fun2do.co.uk
The Green Paint Shop: www.greenshop.co.uk
Hammerite: www.hammerite-diy.com
Homecrafts Direct: www.homecrafts.co.uk
International: www.international-paints.co.uk
Johnstone's Paints (Kalon):
   www.johnstones-paints.co.uk
The Little Greene Paint Company:
   www.thelittlegreene.com
Pébéo (UK): www.pebeo.com
Plasti-kote: www.plastikote.co.uk

Useful contacts

Whether you are looking for low-odour paint or accessories for creating a pirate room, check out the list of useful contacts. We have included customer care numbers, plus website addresses where you can find out more, look for local stockists or shop online.

MURALS, STENCILS & STAMPS

Small and large-scale designs for decorating walls and furniture.

Little Monkey Murals:
 www.makeamuralstencils.com
Motif: www.hennydonovanmotif.co.uk
The English Stamp Company:
 www.englishstamp.com
The Stencil Library: www.stencil-library.co.uk

WALLPAPER, SOFT FURNISHINGS & BORDERS

Co-ordinated wallpaper and soft furnishings ranges, plus children's borders.

Anna French: www.annafrench.co.uk
Coloroll: www.coloroll.net
Crown Wallcoverings: www.wallpapers-uk.com
Graham & Brown: www.grahambrown.com
Harlequin: www.harlequin.uk.com
Laura Ashley: www.lauraashley.com
Osborne & Little: www.osborneandlittle.com
Readyroll (HA Interiors): www.hainteriors.com
Wilman Interiors: www.wilman.co.uk

STORAGE & DETAILS

Clothes and shoe storage, plus neat extras and clever stowaways.

Cotswold Company: www.cotswoldco.com
The Holding Company:
 www.theholdingcompany.co.uk
Lakeland Limited: www.lakelandlimited.com
Wheesh.com: www.wheesh.com

RADIATOR COVERS

Flatpack and custom-made designs to turn radiators into a feature.

Amber Radiator Covers:
 www.amberradiatorcovers.co.uk
Jali: www.jali.co.uk
Johnny Egg: www.johnnyegg.com

FURNITURE

Bunks, wardrobes and other essentials for equipping a bedroom.

AM.PM: www.redoute.co.uk
Great Little Trading Company: www.gltc.co.uk
Ikea: www.ikea.com
John Lewis Direct: www.johnlewis.com
JoJo Maman Bébé:
 www.jojomamanbebe.co.uk
Mothercare: www.mothercare.com
Next: www.next.co.uk
Stompa: www.stompa.co.uk
Urchin: www.urchin.co.uk
Vertbaudet: www.vertbaudet.co.uk

a b c d e
f g h i j k
l m n o p
q r s t u
v w x y z

TEMPLATES

A B C D E
F G H I J K
L M N O P
Q R S T U
V W X Y Z

Index

First published in 2006 by
New Holland Publishers (UK) Ltd
London · Cape Town · Sydney · Auckland

Garfield House, 86–88 Edgware Road
London W2 2EA
United Kingdom
www.newhollandpublishers.com

80 McKenzie Street
Cape Town 8001
South Africa

Level 1, Unit 4, 14 Aquatic Drive
Frenchs Forest, NSW 2086
Australia

218 Lake Road
Northcote, Auckland
New Zealand

ISBN   1 84537 408 8

Senior Editor: Corinne Masciocchi
Design: Isobel Gillan
Production: Hazel Kirkman
Editorial Direction: Rosemary Wilkinson

1 3 5 7 9 10 8 6 4 2

Reproduction by Pica Digital, Singapore
Printed and bound by Times Offset, Malaysia